THE GREAT BIG BOOK OF MAGIC TRICKS

Published in the United States by
QEB Publishing, Inc.
3 Wrigley, Suite A
Irvine, CA 92618

A CIP record for this book is available
from the library of Congress.

ISBN 978-1-60992-697-7

Printed and bound in China

Author Joe Fullman
Managing Editor Amanda Askew
Designer Jackie Palmer
Illustrator Mark Turner for Beehive Illustrations

Picture credits
Alamy Mary Evans Picture Library 75, Mary Evans
Picture Library 99 and 103
Corbis Bettmann 17, Justin Lane/epa 25, Tony Korody/
Sygma 29, Bettmann 38, Hulton-Deutsch Collection 50,
Reuters 67, Bettmann 71, Christopher Farina 110
Cups and Balls Museum 35
Getty Images Time & Life Pictures 19, 33, Hulton
Archive/ Stringer 43, Hulton Archive/ Stringer 45, Ethan
Miller/Staff 56, Paul Drinkwater/Contributor/WireImage
60, Ethan Miller 79, Matthew Peyton 85, Frederick M
Brown 89, 91, Ethan Miller 106 and 119
Rex Features Brian Rasic 20, Dimitris Legakis 23, 97,
105, Charles Sykes 117
Shutterstock Nadina 11, Donald R Swartz 95
Topham Picturepoint Butler Henrietta/ArenaPAL 31

THE GREAT BIG BOOK OF MAGIC TRICKS

JOE FULLMAN

Contents

Contents

How to use this book

ₕave you ever watched a magician perform an amazing trick and wondered how they did it? Then this is the book for you! Learn how to do more than 50 tricks to entertain and astound your friends and family.

① **Preparation**

Sometimes you will need to prepare something beforehand to make a trick work.

② **New Skills Alert**

As you practise the tricks, you will learn several new skills.

Putting on a show

A good magician is more than just a skilled handler of props. They should also be a storyteller and an entertainer. Props, such as a magic wand and glitter, can help bring a trick to life.

Forcing the cards

ₜhe magician places a sealed envelope on a table. They ask a volunteer to choose a car̶ The volunteer then opens the envelope. Someho̶ the name of their chosen card has been writte̶ on the piece of paper inside!

Preparation
You will need to "stack the deck," so the third card in the deck is the Queen of Diamonds. Write the name of the card on a piece of paper, put it in an envelope and seal it. Place the envelope in your pocket.

1 Anno̶ have mo̶ card you̶ the env̶ place it̶ touch i̶

2 Give the deck of cards a quick "false shuffle" and then hand them to your volunteer. Ask them to deal out the top six cards into two rows of three. The Queen of Diamonds should be in the top row on the right-hand side.

3 a) av̶ b) to̶ te̶

2.6

③ Difficulty rating

The tricks get harder throughout the book, so each trick has been given a rating. One is the easiest and seven is the hardest. The most difficult tricks will take a bit of practise to get right, but the results will be worth it!

④ Stages and illustrations

Step-by-step instructions, as well as illustrations, will guide you through each trick.

⑤ Top Tip!

Hints and tips help you to perform the tricks better!

⑥ Famous magicians and illusions

Find out who are the most exciting and skilful magicians, and what amazing feats they have performed.

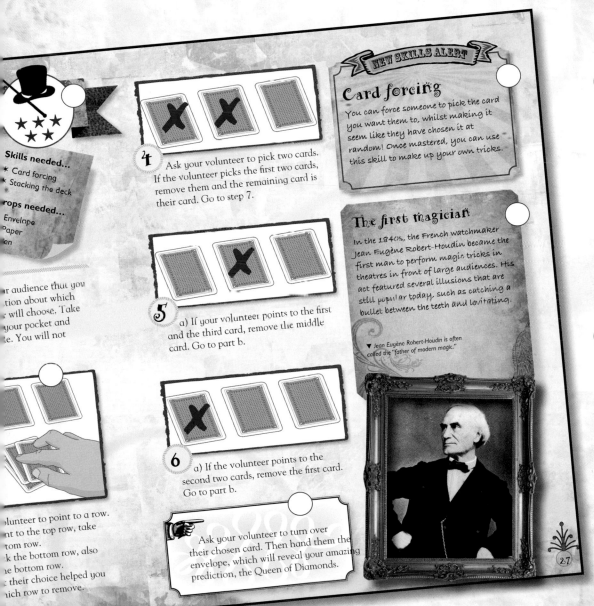

Skills needed...
* Card forcing
* Stacking the deck

Props needed...
Envelope
Paper
en

r audience that you
tion about which
will choose. Take
your pocket and
e. You will not

lunteer to point to a row.
nt to the top row, take
tom row.
k the bottom row, also
e bottom row.
their choice helped you
ich row to remove.

4 Ask your volunteer to pick two cards. If the volunteer picks the first two cards, remove them and the remaining card is their card. Go to step 7.

5 a) If your volunteer points to the first and the third card, remove the middle card. Go to part b.

6 a) If the volunteer points to the second two cards, remove the first card. Go to part b.

☞ Ask your volunteer to turn over their chosen card. Then hand them the envelope, which will reveal your amazing prediction, the Queen of Diamonds.

Card forcing

You can force someone to pick the card you want them to, whilst making it seem like they have chosen it at random! Once mastered, you can use this skill to make up your own tricks.

The first magician

In the 1840s, the French watchmaker Jean Eugène Robert-Houdin became the first man to perform magic tricks in theatres in front of large audiences. His act featured several illusions that are still popular today, such as catching a bullet between the teeth and levitating.

▼ Jean Eugène Robert-Houdin is often called the "father of modern magic."

27

Props you'll need

Card Tricks

- A pack of playing cards, known as the deck. Each pack should contain 54 cards—two Jokers plus four suits of 13 cards. The suits are Spades, Clubs, Diamonds, and Hearts.

- Envelope
- Elastic band
- Handkerchief
- Jacket
- Paper

Coin and Rope Tricks

- Bag
- Coins
- Double-sided scotch tape
- Glass
- Glue
- Handkerchief
- Rope or string
- Light, plastic ball
- Paper
- Pencil
- Scissors
- Scotch tape
- Table
- Thread

Sleight of Hand

- Books
- Chair
- Coins
- Deck of cards
- Dice
- Elastic band
- Envelope
- Grape
- Handkerchief
- Ice cubes
- Jacket or sweater with long sleeves
- Jug of water
- Paper
- Pen
- Pencil
- Plastic cup
- Round-bodied glass
- Ruler
- Scissors
- Sponge
- Sponge ball
- Scotch tape
- Table
- White plastic cup

Mind Tricks

- A pack of playing cards, known as the deck. Each pack should contain 54 cards—two Jokers plus four suits of 13 cards. The suits are Spades, Clubs, Diamonds, and Hearts.

- Banana
- Book or magazine
- Bowl
- Calculator
- Card
- Coins
- Deck of playing cards
- Elastic band
- Soda in a glass bottle
- Glasses
- Jug of water
- Lunchbox
- Metal ring
- Needle and thread
- Packet of wax crayons
- Paper
- Pencils
- Pin
- Stool
- Table
- Toothpicks or cocktail sticks
- Dishwashing liquid
- Watch

CARD TRICKS

Abracadabra!

What better way to start than with the most famous magic word of all? Lay the cards out in the right way and "abracadabra," you will have found your volunteer's card.

1 Deal 21 cards face up into three columns of seven cards. Ask a volunteer to choose one of the cards, but not to tell you which one. Instead, they should tell you which column their card is in. If they choose the eight of Diamonds, they would tell you that they had chosen column three.

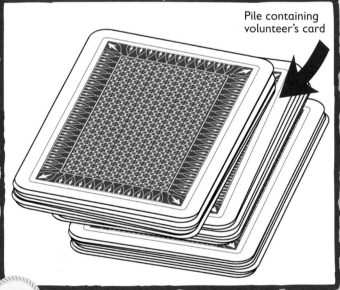

Pile containing volunteer's card

2 Pick up the three columns, keeping the cards in the same order. However, make sure you pick up the column containing your volunteer's card second, so that it sits between the other two columns.

Repeat step two, making sure you keep the cards in each column in order, and that you sandwich the column containing your volunteer's card between the other two columns.

3 Deal out the 21 cards again. Be sure to lay them left to right, rather than up to down. Ask your volunteer which column their card is in now.

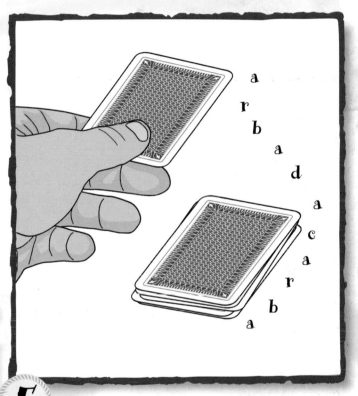

▲ Different countries use different styles of playing cards.

Card magic

The first cards for playing games were created more than 1,000 years ago in China, which is where paper was invented, too. The playing cards that we use today were first made in Egypt about 700 years ago. Traders brought these cards to Europe, where they became very popular. Card games and tricks soon spread around the world.

5 Now deal the cards face down into a pile, spelling out the word "abracadabra," saying a letter for each card you put down. When you get to the final letter "a," hold the card in your hand. Ask your volunteer to tell you the name of their card. Slowly turn over the card in your hand to reveal their chosen card.

Hey presto!

Use the magic words "hey presto" to find your volunteer's card. This trick is special because you do not touch the cards until the end of the trick. Your volunteer does most of the work, making it seem more magical.

Skills needed...
* Card counting
* Misdirection
* Spelling

1 Hand your volunteer a full deck of cards. Ask them to deal all the cards face down into two piles.

2 Ask them to choose one of the piles of cards and look at the bottom card, without letting you see what the card is. They must remember this card.

NEW SKILLS ALERT

Misdirection

For a trick to work, it is important that the audience does not see what is really going on. They should not spot the extra card hidden in your pocket or notice you taking a peek at the bottom card. To do this, magicians use a skill called misdirection—doing things that have nothing to do with the trick! You could tell jokes or wave a magic wand to distract the audience and direct them away from the secrets of the trick.

3 Your volunteer should put their chosen pile on top of the other pile and then square up the deck.

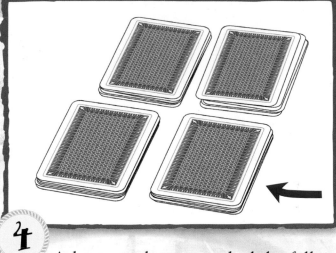

4 Ask your volunteer to deal the full deck face down into four piles. Ask them to look through each pile and tell you which pile contains their card.

Pile containing volunteer's card

5 Pick up the cards, putting the four piles back together to make a whole deck again. Be sure to place the pile containing your volunteer's card on top of the others.

6 Hand the full deck face down to your volunteer and ask them to start dealing out the cards face up. They should spell out the word "presto," saying a letter for each card they put down.

Top Tip!

For step 5, use the new skill of misdirection. Perhaps you could wave a magic wand while you put the piles of cards on top of each other.

7 Take the deck from the volunteer and turn over the top card. Hey presto, it's their chosen card!

An Ace trick

With some clever card preparation, you can magically find all the cards, from Ace to King. An expert false shuffle is guaranteed to astound and amaze your audience.

Skills needed...
* False shuffle
* Memory
* Stacking the deck

Preparation

Before the trick starts, some of the cards need to be arranged into a certain order. This is called "stacking the deck" and your audience must not see you do it.

The first 13 cards of your deck need to be in this order:
Jack, 5, Ace, 8, 10, 2, 6, Queen, 3, 9, 7, 4, King

Make sure that the cards are in different suits. This will make it less obvious to the audience that the cards have been sorted.

1 When your audience is ready, give the deck a quick "false shuffle." This will make it look like you have changed the order of the cards, but will leave the first 13 cards in place, ready for you to begin the trick.

2 Announce to your audience that you are going to sort out the cards. Fan out the cards face up and show them to the audience. The cards will look like they are in a random order.

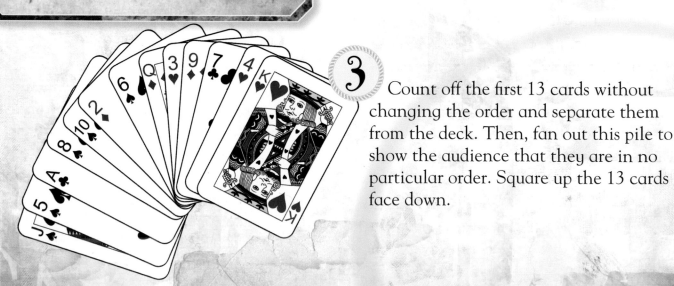

3 Count off the first 13 cards without changing the order and separate them from the deck. Then, fan out this pile to show the audience that they are in no particular order. Square up the 13 cards face down.

Third card is the Ace

Two cards are moved to the back

4 Tell the audience that you can find the Ace. Say "magic number," taking a card from the top of the pile as you say each word and placing it at the back of the 13-card pile. As you take the third card, say "Ace." Place this face up on the table.

5 Next, say the words "magic number," taking a card off the deck for each word and placing them on the bottom of the pack. Say "two" and turn over the third card. It will be the two. Place this on top of the Ace.

6 Continue saying "magic number" and count from three upward, until you reach the King.

False shuffle

- Pick up the deck, as you would to do a normal shuffle.

- Rest the cards in the palm of your hand, with the backs of the cards pointing toward your thumb.

- Holding the cards loosely, take a pile from the middle of the pack, leaving the cards at the front and back.

- Drop the cards in small groups at the back of the pack.

- If you want to leave just the top card in place, pick up a large pile. However, if you want to leave several cards in place, pick up a smaller pile, between the middle and the bottom of the pack.

Mind reading

For this trick, you will need to do a little acting. You are going to pretend that you have "read the mind" of your volunteer. In fact, if you prepare the cards in the right way, this trick will work every time, without you having to do a thing!

Preparation

You will need to "stack the deck" before facing your audience.

The first 11 cards need to be in this order:
6, 5, 4, 3, 2, Ace, Joker, 10, 9, 8, 7

If the cards are in different suits, the audience will not suspect that the cards have been sorted.

1 With your audience in position, give the deck a quick "false shuffle" before you begin the trick to make it look like you have changed the order of the cards.

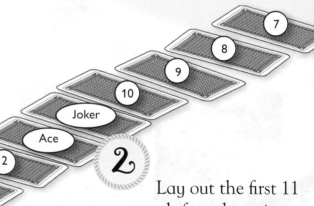

2 Lay out the first 11 cards face down in a row from left to right.

3 Ask your volunteer to move some of the cards from the right-hand side of the row to the left-hand side. They can move as many cards as they like, but they must be sure to move the cards one at a time.

4 Turn your back, so that you cannot see what your volunteer is doing. Ask them to tell you when they have finished moving the cards.

The first magician

In the 1840s, the French watchmaker Jean Eugène Robert-Houdin became the first man to perform magic tricks in theatres in front of large audiences. His act featured several illusions that are still popular today, such as catching a bullet between the teeth and levitating.

▼ *Jean Eugène Robert-Houdin is often called the "father of modern magic."*

5 Turn back and tell them that you are now going to reveal how many cards they moved. In order to make the trick appear more magical, ask your volunteer to think of the number of cards they moved. Tell them you are going to read their mind.

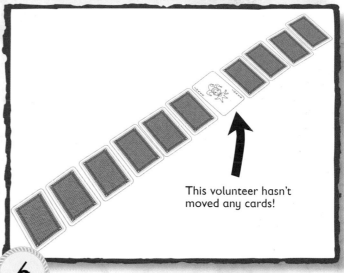

This volunteer hasn't moved any cards!

6 Count seven cards from the left and turn over the card. Whatever the number is on the card, that's the number of cards that have been moved. This works every time, no matter how many cards were moved. If the volunteer decided not to move any cards, you will pick up the Joker.

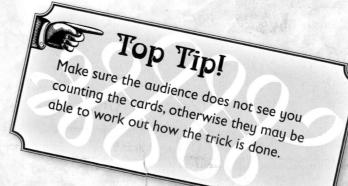

Top Tip!

Make sure the audience does not see you counting the cards, otherwise they may be able to work out how the trick is done.

Aces on top

A volunteer thoroughly mixes up four piles of cards—but each pile ends up with an Ace on top. As long as your volunteer follows your instructions exactly, this trick will never fail. Make sure you do not forget which pile of cards is which!

Preparation

You will need to "stack the deck" before facing your audience. Sort through the cards, find the four Aces, and place them on top of the deck.

1 Face your audience and give the deck a quick "false shuffle" to make it look like you have mixed up the cards.

2 Hand your volunteer the deck of cards. Ask them to divide, or cut, the deck into four roughly equal piles. Remember which pile has the Aces in, or the trick will not work.

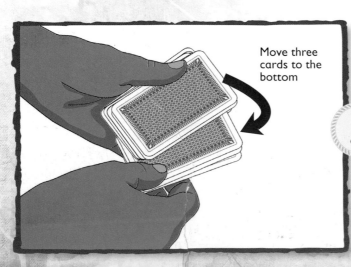

Move three cards to the bottom

3 Ask your volunteer to pick up one of the piles that *does not* contain the Aces. Ask them to take three cards from the top of the pile and to place them on the bottom.

4 Using the cards in their hand, they should then deal one card from the top of the pile onto each of the other piles. Then place the pile face down, next to the others.

5 Repeat steps 3 and 4 with another pile that does not contain the Aces.

6 Repeat steps 3 and 4 with the remaining pile that does not contain the Aces.

7 Repeat steps 3 and 4 with the pile that does contain the Aces.

Street magic

The magician David Blaine has performed many amazing tricks, including pushing a rolled-up dollar bill through a solid coin, levitating, and even bringing a "dead" fly back to life.

▼ *David Blaine often performs tricks on the street to make the illusions seem more real.*

8 Ask your volunteer to turn over the top card on each of the four piles. They are all Aces!

Use the magical power of the elastic band to find your volunteer's card. For the best results, this trick should be performed in front of at least two people.

Skills needed...
* Misdirection
* Sleight of hand

Props needed...
* Elastic band

1 Put the elastic band in your pocket before the start of the trick. Shuffle the cards, fan them out face down, and ask your volunteer to take a card.

2 Ask your volunteer to show the card to the rest of the audience. Tell them that you are going to turn your back while they do this. With your back to the audience, you can now perform "sleight of hand." Turn over the pack so that the cards are all face up. Now turn over the top card so that it is face down.

Practise makes perfect

It takes practise and dedication to become a top card-trick performer. Dynamo is one of the UK's best young magicians. He is very skilled and makes his amazing card tricks seem effortless.

▶ Dynamo skillfully fans out a pack of cards during a trick.

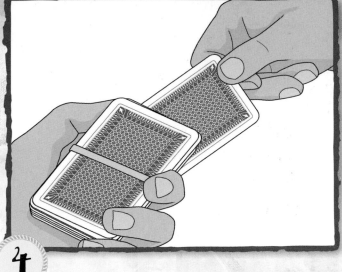

3 Ask your volunteer to hide their chosen card. Turn back to face the audience. Now, take the elastic band from your pocket and wrap it around the deck widthwise.

4 Holding the cards in your left hand with your palm facing upward. Ask the volunteer to put their card face down into the center of the pack.

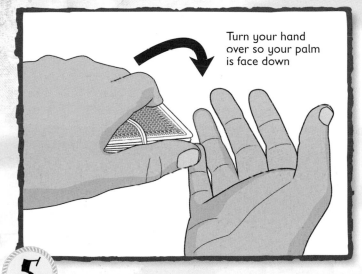

Turn your hand over so your palm is face down

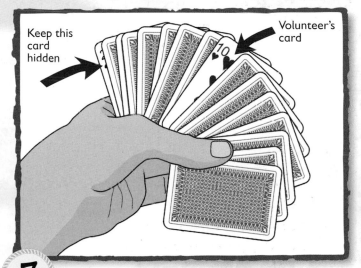

Keep this card hidden

Volunteer's card

5 Now you need to use the new skill of "sleight of hand," so your audience does not see what you are doing. Pass the cards from your left hand to your right hand. As you do this, turn your left hand so that when it reaches your right hand, the palm is facing downward.

6 Holding the pack in your right hand, ask the volunteer to twang the elastic band "to make the magic work."

7 Place the cards back into your left hand—do not turn the deck over. Take off the elastic band. Fan out the cards in your hand until you reach your volunteer's card, which will be face up. Do not fan the cards all the way to the bottom or your audience will see that the bottom card is also face up, and may work out how the trick is done.

Odds and evens

No matter how many times your volunteer shuffles the cards, you always find their chosen card.

Preparation

You need to "stack the deck" so that you have two piles of cards—one of even numbers, and one of odd. Jacks and Kings count as odd, Queens as even. The pile of odd cards will be slightly larger than the pile of evens. Place the pile of even cards on top of the pile of odd cards. Do not square the deck up, but keep the pile of even cards at a slight angle so you can see where the odd cards begin.

1 When your audience is ready, quickly cut your deck into two piles, which you know (but your audience does not) are made up of odd and even cards. It is important to do this smoothly and casually, so that your audience cannot see that you have stacked the deck.

2 Ask a volunteer to shuffle both piles of cards and then choose a pile. Fan out the pile face down and ask them to pick a card and show it only to the audience.

They can then shuffle this pile as many times as they like.

The only even card in a pile of odd cards

3 Ask them to put their chosen card into the other pile.

5 Take the pile, fan through it and find their card. Your volunteer's chosen card will either be the only odd card among the evens, or the only even card among the odds.

Telling a tale

Some magicians like to use acting and stories to make their tricks seem more exciting to their audience. In the show, Tablo, the Italian magician Gaetano Triggiano performs many different illusions, including sawing a woman in half. The illusions all form part of a story about a man searching for his lost love.

▶ Gaetano Triggiano performs a spectacular card trick during his show, Tablo.

Card peeking

For this trick you will need to master a new skill known as "card peeking." This is when you take a quick look at the card on the bottom of the deck, without your audience noticing.

1 Shuffle the cards, remembering to take a quick peek at the bottom card before squaring up the deck.

2 Fan out the cards face down in your hand and ask your volunteer to take one and hold onto it. Square up the deck.

Place new pile on top of the one before

Main deck

3 Place the deck face down on the table and tell your volunteer that you are going to cut the cards into small piles, which you are going to place one on top of the other. Take a small pile off the deck and put it next to the main pile. Repeat this a few times so you end up with five or six small piles.

Top Tip!

Make the cuts small, with just a few cards in each, so that you do not run out of cards before the volunteer puts their card on top in step 4.

4

Ask your volunteer to put their card on top of one of the piles when they feel ready. Then, pick up the main deck and put it top of the pile they choose to put their card on. The card you peeked at earlier is now on top of their card.

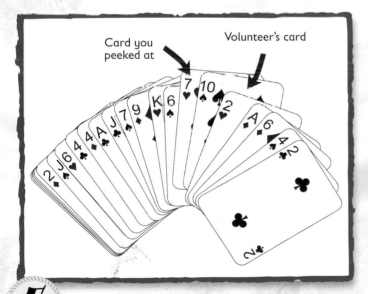

Card you peeked at

Volunteer's card

5

Turn the cards over and fan them out from left to right. Make sure all the cards can be seen. The volunteer's card will be the one to the right of the card you peeked at.

Forcing the cards

The magician places a sealed envelope on a table. They ask a volunteer to choose a card. The volunteer then opens the envelope. Somehow the name of their chosen card has been written on the piece of paper inside!

Skills needed...
* Card forcing
* Stacking the deck

Props needed...
* Envelope
* Paper
* Pen

Preparation

You will need to "stack the deck," so the third card in the deck is the Queen of Diamonds. Write the name of the card on a piece of paper, put it in an envelope and seal it. Place the envelope in your pocket.

1 Announce to your audience that you have made a prediction about which card your volunteer will choose. Take the envelope from your pocket and place it on the table. You will not touch it again.

2 Give the deck of cards a quick "false shuffle" and then hand them to your volunteer. Ask them to deal out the top six cards into two rows of three. The Queen of Diamonds should be in the top row on the right-hand side.

3 Ask your volunteer to point to a row.
a) If they point to the top row, take away the bottom row.
b) If they pick the bottom row, also take away the bottom row.
Pretend that their choice helped you to decide which row to remove.

4 Ask your volunteer to pick two cards. If the volunteer picks the first two cards, remove them and the remaining card is their card. Go to step 7.

Card forcing

You can force someone to pick the card you want them to, whilst making it seem like they have chosen it at random! Once mastered, you can use this skill to make up your own tricks.

5 a) If your volunteer points to the first and the third card, remove the middle card. Go to part b.

b) Ask them to point to another card. Whichever card they choose, remove the first card and give them the card on the right. Go to step 7.

6 a) If the volunteer points to the second two cards, remove the first card. Go to part b.

b) Ask them to point to another card. Whichever card they pick, remove the first card and give them the right-hand card. Go to step 7.

7 Ask your volunteer to turn over their chosen card. Then hand them the envelope, which will reveal your amazing prediction, the Queen of Diamonds.

The pocket

To perform this trick, you will need to wear a jacket with side pockets. You will also have to learn how to do a new piece of "sleight of hand."

Preparation

Before you face your audience, take any two cards from the deck of cards and place them out of sight in the right-hand pocket of your jacket.

1 Hand your volunteer the remainder of the deck of cards. Ask them to shuffle the deck, take three cards off the top and lay them face up on the table.

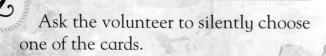

2 Ask the volunteer to silently choose one of the cards.

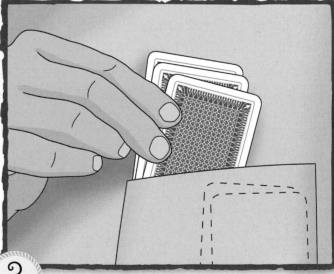

3 Now pick up the three cards. Memorize their order and put them in your right-hand jacket pocket, being sure to keep them separate from the two "secret" cards already there.

4 Ask your volunteer to think of their chosen card. Tell them that you are going to read their mind. After a few moments, say that you think you know what it is and that you are going to get rid of the other two cards.

Popular magician

According to the Guinness Book of World Records, more people have seen the magician David Copperfield perform than any other magician. Copperfield has become world famous for his illusions, many involving well-known landmarks. These have included "levitating over the Grand Canyon" and even "making the Statue of Liberty disappear."

▼ David Copperfield uses his extraordinary skills to levitate a woman.

5 Reach into your pocket and bring out the two "secret" cards, keeping the cards chosen by your volunteer safely in your pocket. Place these two cards face down on the table.

6 Ask your volunteer to name their card. When they do, reach into your pocket, count to the correct card and pull it out. The tricky bit is doing this quickly and easily, so that it does not look like you are counting cards in your pocket. This may take a bit of practise.

The vanishing card

Skills needed...
* Sleight of hand

Props required...
* Handkerchief
* Scissors
* Toothpick or cocktail stick

This trick requires quite a lot of preparation, but the end result is guaranteed to baffle your audience.

Preparation

• Using scissors, cut the toothpick so that it is the same length as one of your cards. Remove the sharp ends.

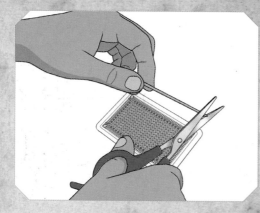

• Tuck the toothpick into the hem of your handkerchief. Make sure it is secure and will not fall out. Place the handkerchief in your pocket.

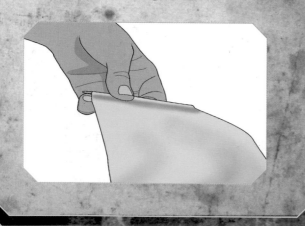

1 Throw a deck of cards onto a table, so that the cards are in a messy pile.

2 Take the handkerchief out of your pocket. Make sure the hem holding the toothpick is facing downward, so that it cannot be spotted by the audience.

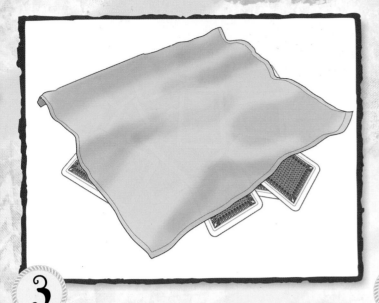

3 Place the handkerchief over the pile of cards. Announce that you are going to make one of the cards disappear.

4 Place your finger and thumb on either end of the toothpick. Pick the toothpick up. To the audience, this will look like you have picked up a card.

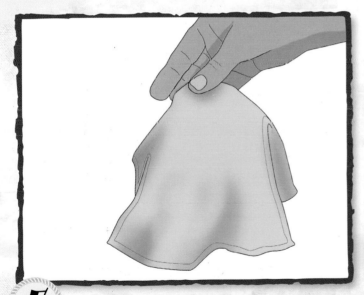

5 Say the magic word, "abracadabra," lift the hanky in the air and quickly transfer your grip from the toothpick to the corner of the handkerchief. Wave the handkerchief around. It will look like the card has vanished. Only you will know that it was never there to begin with.

Card throwing

The magician Ricky Jay can throw a playing card more than 200 feet (60 meters). He can also throw a card with such force that it can pierce the rind of a water melon from more than 10 feet (3 meters) away.

▼ Ricky Jay demonstrates his amazing card skills.

The magic shoe

Tricks always seem much more magical if you can find a new and special way to reveal the chosen card.

Skills needed...
* Card peeking
* False ashuffling
* Sleight of hand

Props needed...
* Handkerchief
* Paper
* Pen
* Shoe

Preparation

Before facing your audience, peek at the top card of the deck. Write the name of the card on a piece of paper, fold it up, and tuck it in your shoe. Place the handkerchief in your pocket.

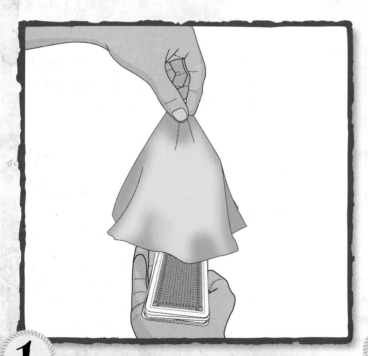

1 To get your audience to believe that you are using mixed up cards, perform a quick "false shuffle." Then, take the deck and hold it in your right hand just above the table. Put the handkerchief over the deck of cards.

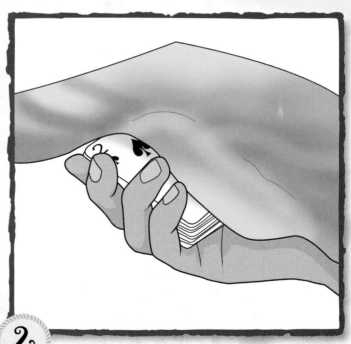

2 As you place the handkerchief over your hand, use your fingers and thumb to turn the deck over so that it is face up. This needs to be done quickly and smoothly, so that your audience does not notice.

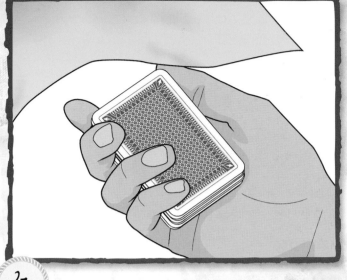

3 Now, ask a volunteer to cut the deck through the handkerchief and to place their pile of cards on the table (still under the handkerchief).

4 Turn the cards in your hand over, so that they are once again face down. The top card will now be the one you looked at earlier. Use your other hand to move your volunteer's pile of cards, so that they cannot inspect it.

5 Give your volunteer the deck of cards in your right hand. Ask them to turn over the top card and say what it is. As they do this, slip off your shoe containing the piece of paper.

6 Ask your volunteer to take the piece of paper out of the shoe and read your prediction. That shoe is magic!

See-through magic

Many magicians perform a trick using cups and balls. However, U.S. magician Jason Latimer performs a special version using see-through glass cups. Even though the balls can be seen by the audience at all times, he still manages to make them disappear and reappear—as if by magic.

▶ *Jason Latimer shows his audience that the props are normal before he astounds them with his trick.*

The lift

This trick is simple, but it will probably take a lot of practise before you feel confident enough to try it in front of an audience.

NEW SKILLS ALERT

Double lift

You need to pick up two cards in such a way that it looks like you have only picked up one.

• Use your thumb and first two fingers to find the top two cards.

• As you lift the cards press down slightly so that the cards bend a little. The cards will stick together and make it look as if you have only lifted one card.

1

Square up the deck and perform the double lift. Show the card underneath to the audience. They will think that they are looking at the top card.

2

Put the cards back on top of the deck.

3 Now take the top card and put it on the bottom of the deck. The audience will think you are moving the card that they saw.

4 Square up the deck and announce you are going to make the bottom card rise to the top of the pack. Snap your fingers over the deck.

The oldest trick

No one knows how long magic tricks have been around, but it is believed to be many thousands of years. Some archeologists think that a painting on the wall of a tomb from ancient Egypt shows the earliest image of a magic trick. In the picture, a figure appears to performing an illusion using a series of cups.

▼ Were these ancient Egyptians performing the cup and ball trick?

5 Now turn over the top card. It will look to your audience as if the card has "magically" jumped from the bottom of the deck to the top!

Simple skills to master

In addition to learning the skills mentioned in the "New Skills Alert" boxes, it is also important to practise the following techniques if you want to become a top magician.

Card counting

For some tricks, the only skill you need is the ability to count—making sure you have laid out or picked up the correct number of cards and then placed them in their correct order.

Card peeking

To "peek" is to take a secret look at a card, allowing you to memorize its number and suit without your audience realizing what you are doing.

Cutting

To "cut" a pack is to roughly divide it by taking a pile off the top.

Memory

Having a good memory is vital if you want to be a good magician—tricks often have several stages that need to be remembered clearly and in the correct order.

Observation

A keen eye is one of a magician's most vital skills. You have to be aware of what is going on at all times.

Sleight of hand

You need to be able to move something secretly with your hands in such a way that the audience thinks you are doing something else.

Spelling

For some tricks you will need to spell out a word for the trick to work. Learn how to spell the word—and practise spelling it—before performing the trick or you may make a mistake.

Stacking the deck

Stacking the deck means to secretly arrange the cards, usually before the trick begins, so some of them are in a certain order—which the magician knows, but the audience does not.

COIN AND ROPE
TRICKS

The magic hole

This simple challenge is a good way to get started. Hand your volunteer the piece of paper and the larger coin. Ask them to try to pass the larger coin through the hole without tearing the paper. When they give up, show them how it is done.

Props needed...

- ❺ Piece of paper about 5x5 inches (12x12 centimeters)
- ❺ Scissors
- ❺ Two coins of slightly different sizes, such as a dime and a nickel

The most famous magician in the world

Born in Hungary in 1874, Eric Weiss moved to the U.S. with his family when he was just four years old. There he would grow up to become the best-known magician in the world, performing under the stage name, Harry Houdini. He was particularly famed for his feats of escapology—he escaped from many devices, including handcuffs, chains, straitjackets, and water-filled tanks.

▶ Harry Houdini escapes from a straitjacket while suspended above a crowd of people in New York City.

Preparation

- Take the smaller coin, place it in the center of your piece of paper and draw a circle around it.

- Using scissors, carefully cut out around the circle to make a hole.

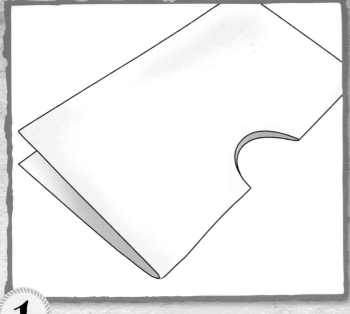

1 Fold the paper in half.

2 Drop the larger coin into the pouch formed by the paper.

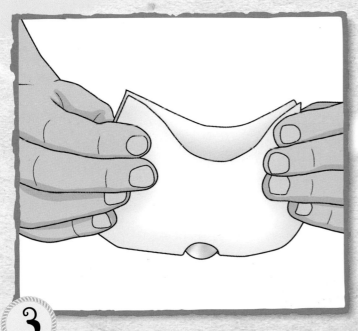

3 Push the ends of the paper together. This will increase the size of the hole.

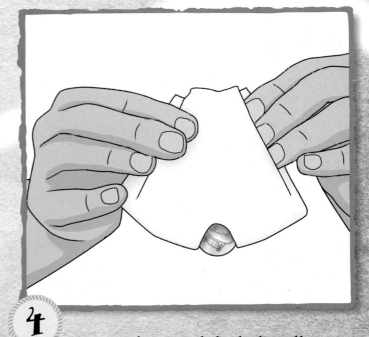

4 Keep pushing and the hole will eventually be big enough for the larger coin to fall through, without tearing the paper. Magic!

Cross-armed knot

This challenge is a great one to try at parties. Take the length of rope and hand it to a volunteer from your audience. Ask them to grip one end of the rope with one hand and the other end with the other hand. Now challenge them to tie a knot in the rope without releasing their grip. When they give up, show them how it is done.

Props needed...
* Length of rope or string, about 2 feet (60 centimeters) long
* Table

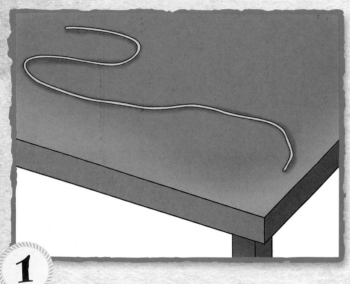

1 Lay the rope in front of you on a flat surface, such as a table.

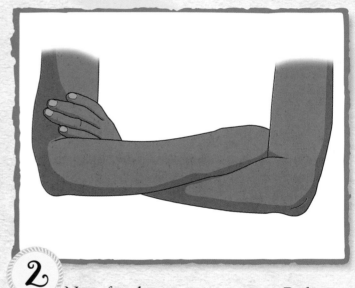

2 Now for the important part. Before you pick up the rope, fold your arms, so that one hand is resting on top, and one hand is tucked underneath.

Top Tip!

Telling jokes is a great way of putting your audience at ease. Plus, it distracts them from concentrating too hard on what you are doing.

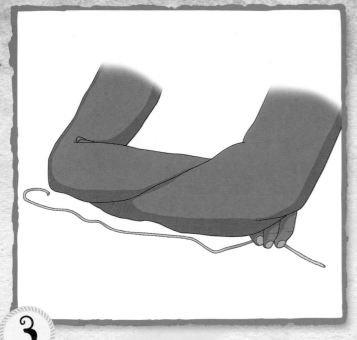

3 With your arms folded, lean forward and pick up one end of the rope using the hand that is tucked underneath.

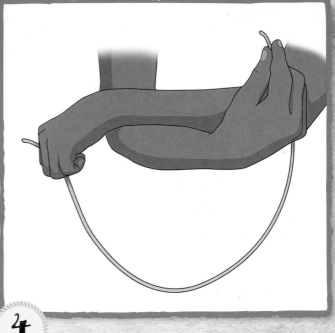

4 Grab the other end of the rope with the hand that is resting on top.

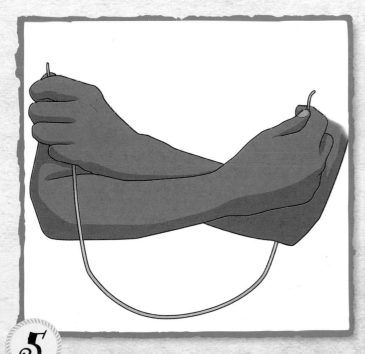

5 Slowly uncross your arms, while still holding on to the rope.

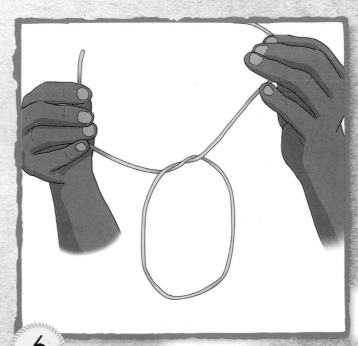

6 As your hands pass by each other, a loop will form in the center of the rope. Keep pulling and you will have a knot —without ever letting go of the rope.

The coin bag

For this trick, you need to do a little acting to convince your audience that you are a magical master!

Props needed...
* Bag
* Coins, each with a different date
* Table

Preparation

Before facing your audience, put the coins into your bag and then put the bag into the refrigerator for a few minutes. This will make the coins slightly colder than room temperature—which is important for the trick to work. Don't make them so cold that your audience will notice.

1 Place the bag of coins on the table in front of you. Ask a volunteer from the audience to approach the table.

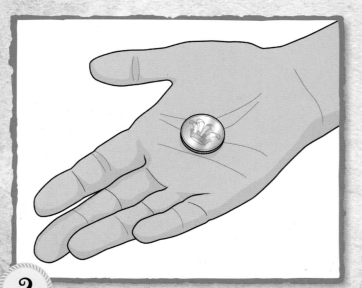

2 Now turn your back and ask them to pick a coin from the bag. Tell them to look at the date on the coin and remember it.

3 Tell them to close their fingers around the coin and to think of the coin's date. Turn back and tell your volunteer that you are going to try to read their mind. Stare at their face, as if you are trying to read their thoughts.

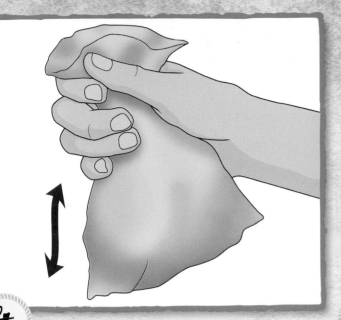

4 Ask them to put the coin back into the bag and to give it a thorough shake to mix all the coins up.

5 The secret of this trick is body temperature. By holding the coin in their hand, your volunteer will have made it much warmer than all the other coins. All you have to do now is reach inside the bag and pick out the coin that feels warmer than the rest.

6 Pull out their coin and tell them the date. Now ask your volunteer to tip all the other coins onto the table and to check them, so they can see that all the coins have different dates.

Magic in the family

In the 19th century, the British magician John Maskelyne performed a well-known magic act with his partner George Cooke at a specially built London theater, the Egyptian Hall. They were the first people to perform the illusion of levitation. Maskelyne's son Nevil was also a magician, as was his son, Jasper. In World War II, Jasper used his talents to trick the enemy by creating fake tanks and planes.

▶ A ticket for Maskelyne and Cooke's famous magic act, which they used to perform twice a day at the Egyptian Hall Theater.

The knot is gone!

★★★

For this trick, you will need to learn how to tie a "false knot"—a knot that looks like a real knot, but will untie itself when you pull on both ends of the rope. You will need to practise tying the knot before performing the trick, so you can do it quickly and easily.

Props needed...

* Handkerchief
* Length of rope or string

NEW SKILLS ALERT

How to tie a false knot

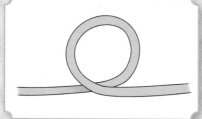

1 Take your rope and twist it into a circle.

2 Now, form a loop in the rope, just to the right of the circle.

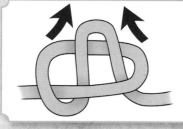

3 Take the loop and tuck it up into the circle.

4 Take hold of the top of the loop with the finger and thumb of your right hand. Grip the rope to the right of the loop with your other three fingers. Now, use your left hand to pull the left end of the rope, so that the circle wraps tightly around the loop.

1 Take out a length of rope and a handkerchief and show them to your audience. Ask a volunteer to examine them closely, so they can see there is nothing unusual about them.

2 Take the rope back and tie a false knot in it, in view of the audience.

4 Pull gently on the rope while the knot is under the handkerchief.

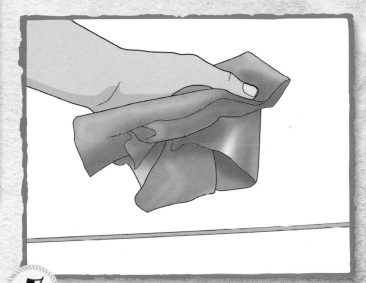

3 Holding the rope by its ends, ask your volunteer to place the handkerchief over the knot.

5 Ask your volunteer to take the handkerchief off the rope. The knot has magically disappeared.

Bringing back magic

Magic has not always been popular. After a boom in the late 19th and early 20th centuries, magic shows began to attract fewer people following the invention of film and television. Magic came to be seen as boring and old fashioned.

▶ Doug Henning was a Canadian magician who helped make magic popular again in the 1970s with his energetic performance and colorful clothes.

The vanishing coin

Amaze your audience by magically making a coin disappear and reappear.

Preparation

1 Take one of the large pieces of paper and lay it down flat.

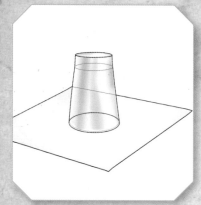

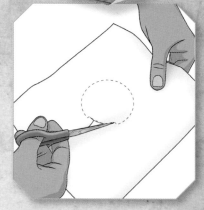

2 Place your glass on top of it with the mouth facing downward.

3 Using a pencil, trace around the outline of the glass.

4 Carefully cut along the pencil line, so that you are left with a circle of paper.

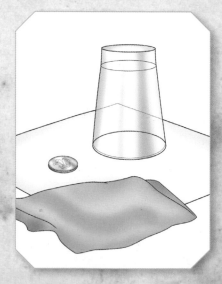

5 Line the rim of your glass with glue and stick the paper circle on top. Once the glue is dry, cut off any extra paper.

6 Before your audience is in position, place the coin, the prepared glass, and the handkerchief on top of the other piece of paper.

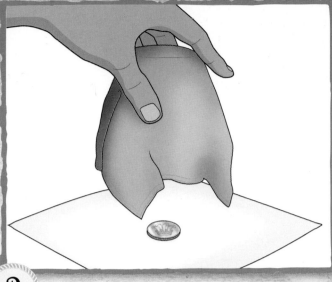

1 Announce to your audience that you are going to make the coin disappear. Now pick up the handkerchief and place it over the glass.

2 Place the handkerchief and glass over the coin that is sitting on the paper.

4 Put the handkerchief back over the glass.

3 Take away the handkerchief to show that the coin has vanished, or so it will seem to your audience. Of course, you know that the coin is just hidden by the paper stuck to the glass, which is the same color as the paper below.

5 Lift up the handkerchief and the glass to reveal that the coin has now magically reappeared.

Top Tip!
Use a thin coin, so that its shape does not show through the paper.

One-handed knot

In this trick, you will show your audience a length of rope, take it in one hand, make a few quick movements and magically you will have tied a knot, using just one hand. You need to practise, but the amazed looks on your friends' faces will make the effort worth it!

Props needed...

* Length of rope or string

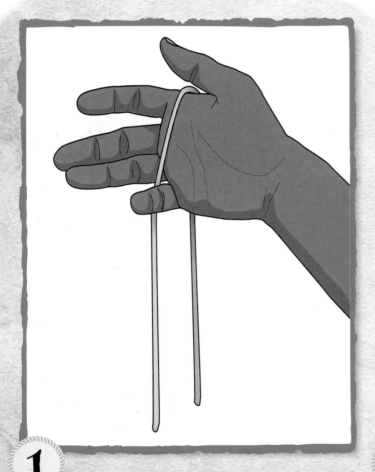

1 Drape the rope over your hand so that one end is hanging between your third finger and your little finger.

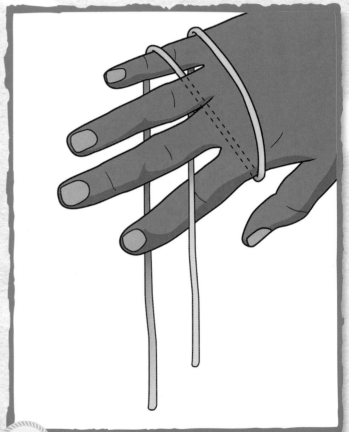

2 Now turn your hand the other way up, and then catch the other end between your first and second fingers.

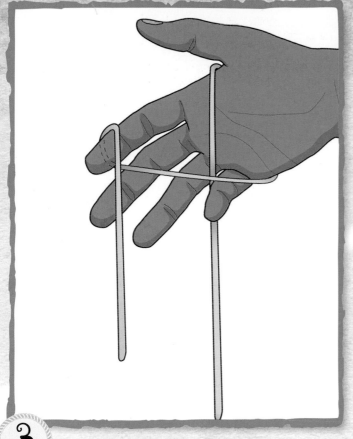

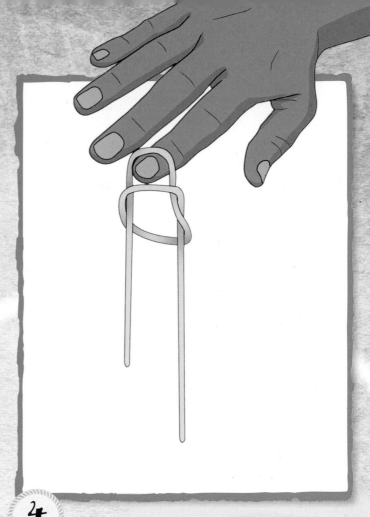

3 Turn your hand again, so your thumb is once again facing up.

4 Keeping hold of the rope between your first and second finger, point your fingers down, and let the rest of the rope slide off your hand.

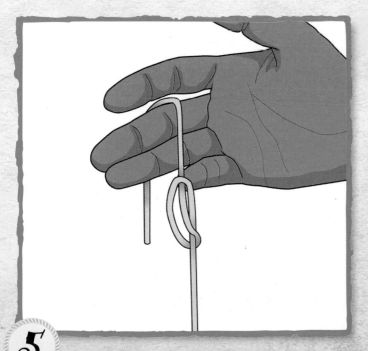

Top Tip!

Once you have mastered the technique, you can try it with the other hand. See if you can tie two knots in a long piece of rope at the same time.

5 As the rope slides off, it will tie itself into a knot.

The sticky nail

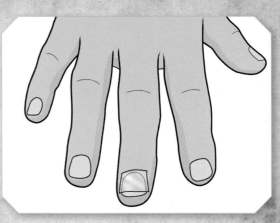

Use a small piece of scotch tape to make it look like a coin has disappeared.

Props needed...

* Coin
* Double-sided scotch tape

On the high wire

He may not have been a magician, but "The Great Blondin" performed many amazing feats during his career. His speciality was tightrope walking. In his act, he would walk on stilts, turn somersaults, and even carry someone on his back—all while balanced on a high rope. He became world famous in 1859 when he crossed Niagara Falls, on a tightrope 1,100 feet (335 meters) in length.

▼ Charles Blondin, the French acrobat, performs a tightrope walk high above Niagara Falls

Preparation

• Take a small piece of double-sided scotch tape and place it on the nail that is nearest to the coin.

• Put the coin in your pocket.

50

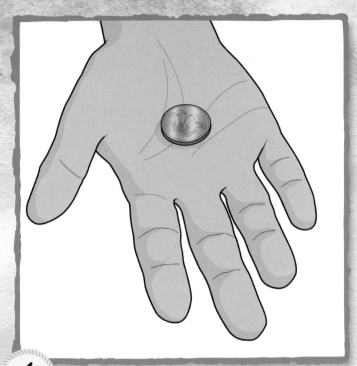

1 Show your empty hands to the audience. Keep your nails turned toward you, so that the audience cannot see the piece of tape. Take the coin from your pocket and place it in the palm of your hand.

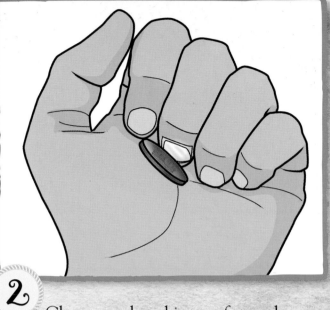

2 Close your hand into a fist and press the nail with the scotch tape onto the coin.

3 Wave your other hand over your closed fingers in a "magical" way to block your audience's view.

5 To get rid of the coin, put your hand in your pocket and let the coin fall off your finger.

4 Now, quickly open your hand to show that the coin has disappeared. Only you will know that it is stuck to your nail.

Top Tip!
The lighter in weight the coin is, the easier this trick will be.

Two into one

In this trick, you will use some simple sleight of hand to stun your audience—by making two pieces of rope become one!

Props needed...

* Two lengths of rope—one long, one short

NEW SKILLS ALERT

Sleight of hand

One of the most important skills a magician can learn, sleight of hand means to move something without your audience seeing what you are doing. When you hide something in your hand or pretend to put something in your pocket, you are performing sleight of hand.

Preparation

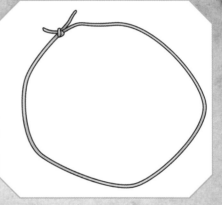

• Take the long piece of rope and tie the ends together into a knot, forming a loop.

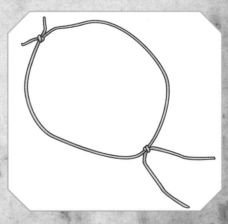

• Now take the smaller piece of rope and tie it around the longer piece on the opposite side to the first knot. This will make it look like the loop is made of two short pieces of rope tied together.

Top Tip!

Make sure you don't tie the short rope around the long rope too tightly, or you will not be able to slide it off.

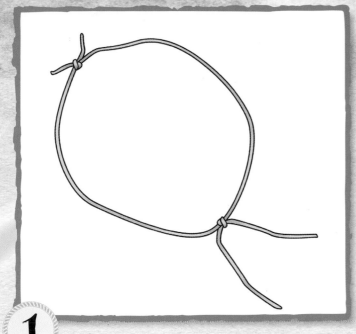

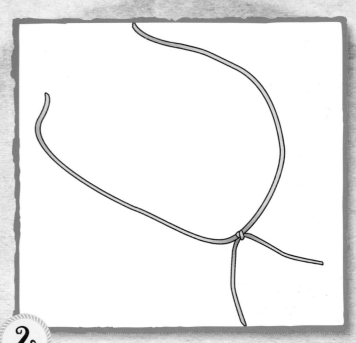

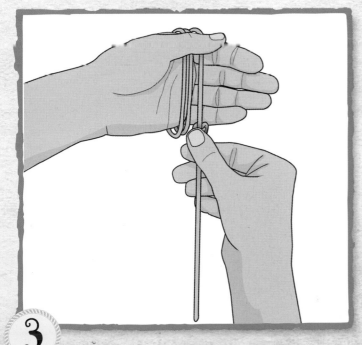

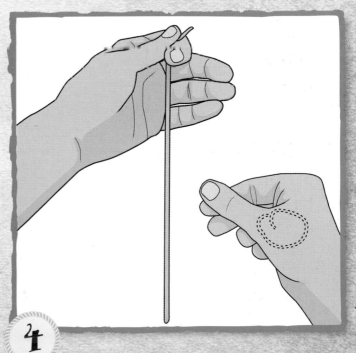

1 Take out your prepared rope and tell your audience that it is a loop made from two short pieces of rope tied together. Only you will know that it is actually one long piece of rope and one short piece of rope.

2 Tell your audience that the ropes were tied together using two types of knot. The first is just a normal knot. As you say this, undo the knot holding the ends of the long piece of rope together.

3 Start winding the rope around your hand. As you wind, slide the knot made from the short piece of rope off into your winding hand.

4 Keeping the short piece of rope hidden in one hand, show your audience that the two "short pieces" of rope have now become one!

Magic paper

You take out a coin and place it in the center of a small square of paper. You fold the paper around the coin, say a few magic words, and then tear the paper into pieces. The coin has vanished. But how?

1 Place your coin in the center of the paper.

2 Now fold the bottom edge up until it is about a quarter of an inch (5 millimeters) from the top.

3 Fold the right-hand side of the paper behind the coin.

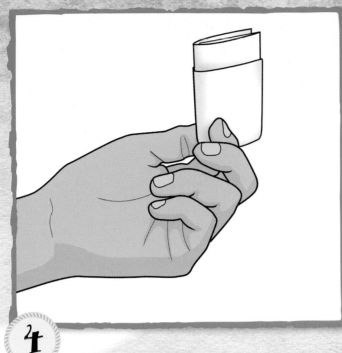

4 Fold the left-hand side of the paper behind the coin.

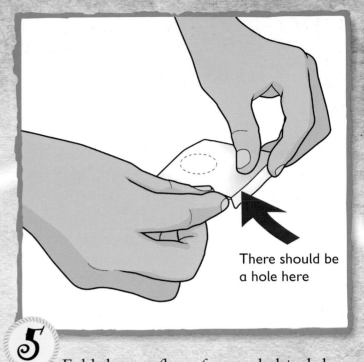

There should be a hole here

5 Fold the top flap of paper behind the coin. To the audience this will look like the coin has been completely sealed in. In fact, if you have folded the paper correctly, there will be hole at the top.

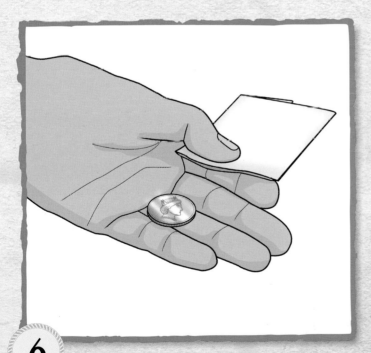

6 You will now need to perform sleight of hand. Turn the paper upside down and, without letting the audience see, allow the coin to fall into your hand.

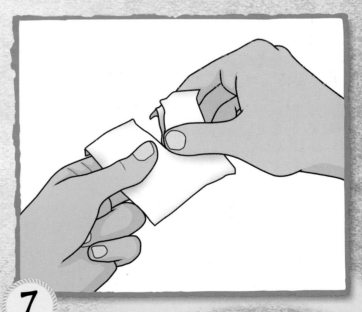

7 Keeping the coin hidden in your hand, tear the paper in half and then in half again. The coin has vanished.

Balancing the ball

In this trick, it will look like you are rolling a ball along a piece of rope. In fact you are going to get some invisible assistance.

Props needed...

* Length of rope
* Length of thin thread, the same length as the rope
* Light, plastic ball
* Table

Preparation

Before performing this trick, you need to attach a length of thread to the rope.

When the magic doesn't work

Even professional magicians sometimes get it wrong. In 2007, in Las Vegas, magician Nathan Burton attempted to spend 24 hours trapped inside an ice sculpture. Unfortunately the day on which he chose to perform his trick was so hot that the ice quickly began to melt and the attempt was called off after just a few hours, leaving Burton feeling embarrassed—and wet!

▼ Burton peers out from his rapidly melting ice prison.

Top Tip!

Keep a distance from your audience when you perform this trick, so they cannot spot the thread. Do not let anyone inspect the rope after the trick.

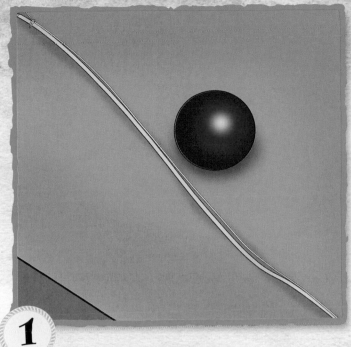

1

Lay the length of rope on a table and place a plastic ball in front of it.

2

When you lift the ball, you are going to pick it up between the rope and the thread—it will look to the audience as if you are just using the rope.

3

Impossible as it seems, start rolling the ball backward and forward along the rope. Make sure your audience does not look too closely.

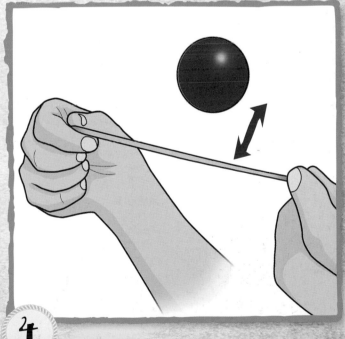

4

Watch how amazed your audience is as you throw the ball in the air and catch it again on the rope.

The handshake

Watch your friends gasp in amazement as a coin appears to travel right through your hand.

Props needed...
* Coin

1 Place a coin in the palm of your hand and close your fingers around it, making a fist.

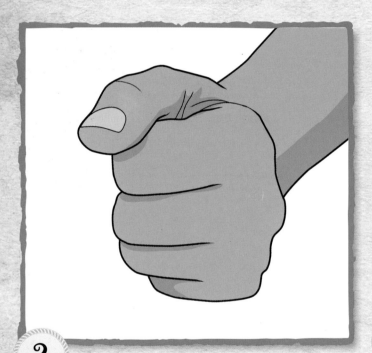

2 Turn your fist over, so that your thumb is facing upward.

3 Take your other hand and place it over your fist, so that the fingers are at the front, facing your audience.

4 Say the magic word "abracadabra" and start shaking your hands up and down.

Top Tip!
The quicker you can perform this trick, the more convincing it will seem.

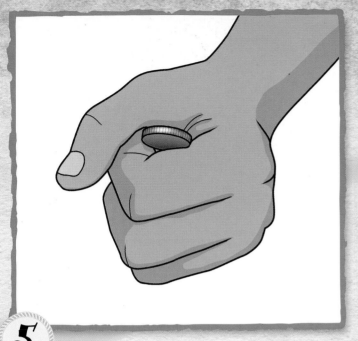

5 Make sure the top hand is pressing down tightly on the one below, but loosen the grip of the hand holding the coin. As you shake your hands, the coin will pop up between the thumb and first finger of your fist.

6 Keep shaking and use the top hand to slide the coin on top of your other hand, out of sight of your audience. The shaking will make it difficult for the audience to see exactly what you are doing.

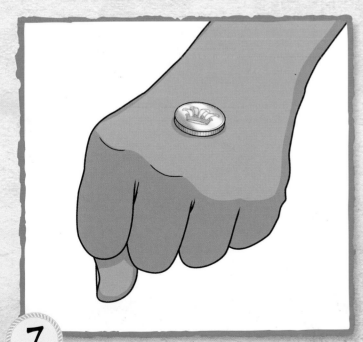

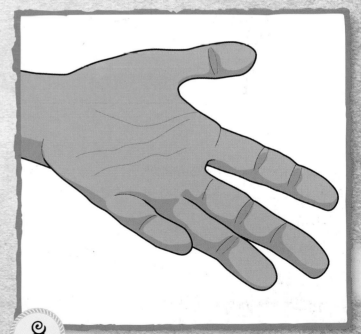

7 Take your top hand away to show that the coin is now sitting on top of the lower hand.

8 Pick up the coin and turn over your hand, showing the audience that the coin is not in your hand—it has traveled all the way through!

The magic rope

Holding a long length of rope in your hand, you cut the rope in half, making two short ropes. You say the magic word, "abracadabra," and release your hand to reveal that the rope has been magically restored to its full length! Cue audience amazement. You will need to practise sleight of hand to get this trick to work.

Props needed...
* Long length of rope
* Scissors
* Short length of rope
* Scotch tape

Preparation

• Before you start this trick, take the short length of rope and curl it into a narrow loop.

• Stick the ends together with scotch tape, so it holds its shape. Then hide the loop in your hand.

• Put the long piece of rope in your jacket pocket.

The capital of magic

More magic shows are performed every year in the city of Las Vegas than anywhere else in the world. Many of the city's casinos have large theaters where lavish magic shows—complete with explosions, light shows and performing animals—are put on. Several of the world's most popular magicians have performed here, including David Copperfield, Lance Burton, and Criss Angel.

◀ Lance Burton levitates actress Pamela Anderson during his Las Vegas magic show.

1 Keep the hand holding the short length of rope hanging casually by your side. Take the long length of rope out of your pocket. Hold it by one end to show the audience that it is one long piece of rope. Then, take hold of it in the middle, so that it hangs as two strands.

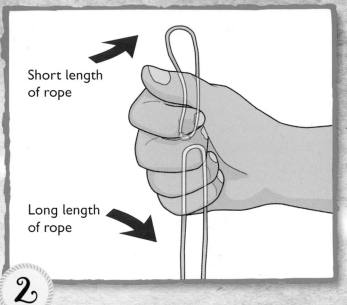

Short length of rope

Long length of rope

2 Pass the rope up through the bottom of your other hand. Feed it about half way up, and leave it there. Now transfer your grip to the small loop already in your hand. Pull the end of this small loop out of the top of your hand.

3 Ask a volunteer to carefully cut through the small loop sticking out the top of your hand. The audience will think they have cut the long rope.

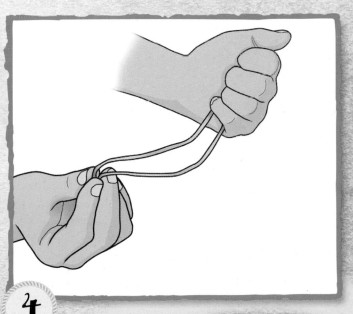

4 Wave your free hand over the rope. This will obscure your audience's view. Now tuck the cut ends of the small loop back into your hand and pull out the long length of rope, showing that it is whole again.

The sticky hand

This clever piece of sleight of hand will take a bit of practise to get right.

Props needed...
* Coin
* Glue

Preparation

Before facing your audience, put a small amount of glue onto the back of your hand.

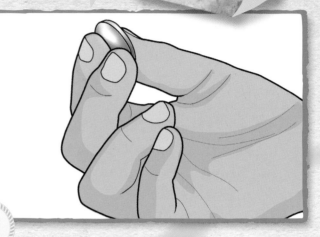

1 Hold the coin between your thumb and first two fingers of your non-sticky hand, and show it to your audience.

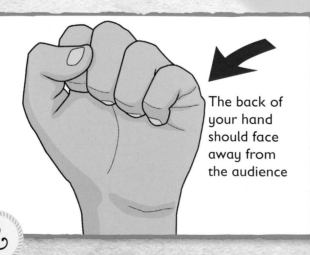

The back of your hand should face away from the audience

2 Make a fist with your sticky hand. Hold the fist up, so the back of your hand is facing you.

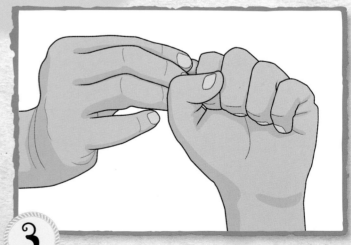

3 Tell the audience that you are going to put the coin inside your fist. Using your thumb and the first two fingers of your non-sticky hand, place the coin at the opening of your fist.

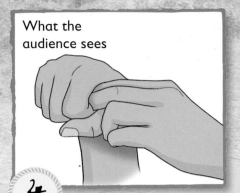

What the audience sees

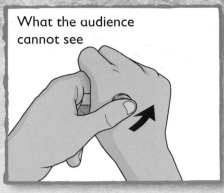

What the audience cannot see

4 Push your first two fingers into your fist as if you were pushing the coin inside. These fingers will cover the audience's view of your thumb.

At the same time, use your thumb to push the coin, out of sight of your audience, onto the back of your hand where it will stick to the glue.

5 With the coin in position, pull your fingers out and wave them over the closed fist. Say the magic word, "abracadabra."

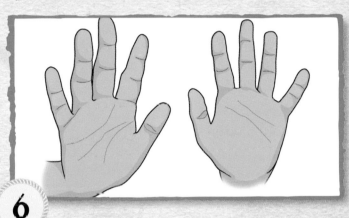

6 Open you hands, palm up to the audience, to show that the coin has vanished.

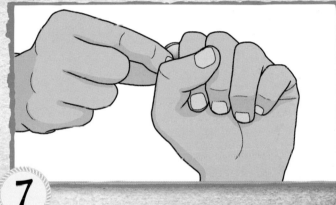

7 Now announce that you are going to bring the coin back. Close your hand back into a fist, and place the two fingers of your non-sticky hand inside.

8 Slowly remove your fingers. As you do, use your thumb to slide the coin from the back of your hand into your fist.

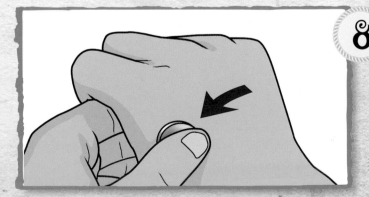

9 Once the coin is inside your fist take your other hand away, open your palm and reveal the coin.

The greatest illusion

The Indian rope trick is one of the world's most famous illusions—or is it the world's greatest fake?

In the trick, a magician throws a rope up into the air. However, instead of falling back to the ground, the rope stands stiff and upright. The magician's assistant then climbs the rope and, when he reaches the top, disappears, at which point the rope collapses. After a few moments, the assistant then reappears back on the ground.

Supposedly the trick has been performed in India for centuries. However, some people doubt whether it really exists, believing stories about the trick to be " tall tales." Certainly there is no film or television footage of anyone having performed the trick. It has even been claimed that the trick was invented by a U.S. newspaper reporter in 1890 to get publicity for his paper.

The Magic Circle, a society of British magicians, became so convinced that the trick was a fake that they offered a large cash prize to anyone who could recreate it at their headquarters in London, England. No one ever claimed the prize.

▲ A magician's assistant begins to climb the rope, but will they disappear?

SLEIGHT OF HAND

The wobbly pencil

This trick is a simple optical illusion. The secret is learning how to move the pencil at just the right speed to make it look rubbery. Practise this before performing the trick in front of an audience.

1

Ask a volunteer from the audience to inspect the pencil to make sure there is nothing unusual about it.

2

Tell your volunteer that you are going to turn the pencil into rubber. Wave your hands over the pencil as if you are performing a magic spell, and say the magic word, "abracadabra."

Hold the pencil one inch from the end

Top Tip!

The more you act as if you have "magic powers," the more your audience will believe you.

3

Now, using your thumb and first finger, pick up the pencil about one inch (2 centimeters) from the pointed end and hold it horizontally.

4

Holding the pencil lightly in front of you, start to wiggle it up and down. The pencil will appear to go wobbly.

5

After a while, stop wiggling the pencil and wave your free hand over it to make it solid again. Hand the pencil back to your friend, so they can see it is, once again, just an ordinary pencil.

Breaking free

Escapology is a type of magic in which a magician breaks free from something holding them. This can be anything from ropes or handcuffs to chains and straitjackets. Escapologists often rely on sleight of hand to perform their tricks—hiding keys or tools in their hands to help them to escape.

▶ An escapologist from Georgia, Zurab Vadachkoria is handcuffed and locked inside a water-filled tank. He escapes unscathed four minutes later.

instant ice

You pick up the plastic cup, pour in some water, turn it over and, "hey presto," a couple of ice cubes come tumbling out. The magic for this simple trick is all in the preparation. The clever bit is making sure your audience cannot see what you are really doing.

Props needed...

* Ice cubes
* Jug of water
* Scissors
* Small piece of sponge
* White plastic cup

Preparation

• Cut a small piece of sponge, just slightly bigger than the base of your cup.

• Make sure the sponge is squashed tightly inside the cup and will not fall out when you turn over the cup.

• Now put a couple of ice cubes on top of the sponge.

1 Show the plastic cup to the audience and tell them that you are going to make instant ice cubes.

Top Tip!
When you show the cup, tilt it a little toward the audience, but make sure you do not tip it too far, otherwise they will see the ice cubes.

2 Pick up the jug and pour an inch of water into the cup. Unseen by the audience, the sponge will soak up the water.

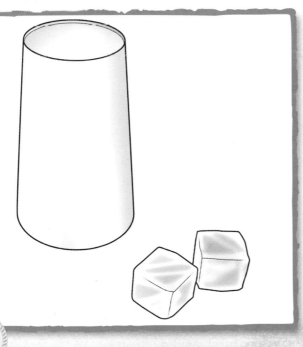

3 Wave your hand over the cup, say the magic word, "abracadabra," and turn over the cup, tipping out the ice cubes. To the audience, it will look like the water has instantly frozen.

4 Finish the trick by crumpling the cup and throwing it away. This will stop the audience from examining it and working out how the trick is done.

The grape olympics

★ ★

You will need to be very careful when performing this trick, as you will be handling a glass. Make sure there is an adult present before you begin the grape olympics!

Preparation

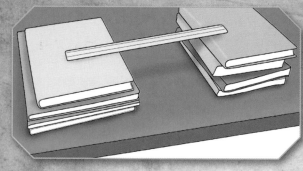

• On a tabletop, use the books and ruler to make a jump.

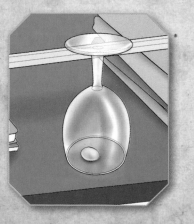

• Place your grape on one side of the jump, and your glass on top of the grape.

1

Bet your friend that they cannot get the grape to travel over the jump without tipping over the glass or touching the grape with their hands. When they give up, show them how it is done.

**Top Tip!**
This is a very good trick for improving your "hand-eye coordination"—an important part of learning how to do sleight-of-hand tricks.

2
Grip the glass and start spinning it around very quickly in small circles. This will create something known as "centrifugal force," which will make the grape spin around inside the glass.

3
Keep on spinning and lift the glass up and over the jump—without the grape falling out—and put it down on the other side.

Little and large

Some magicians perform small tricks using cards or coins. Others work on a much bigger scale. Harry Blackstone was a U.S. magician who specialized in large illusions, including "sawing a woman in half" and "levitation." Blackstone's most famous trick, however, used a simple light bulb that he would magically make glow and float over the heads of his audience.

▶ Harry Blackstone performs an illusion in which he appears to pull his assistant's head up through a tube.

Two into one

Amaze your audience as you turn two small paper rings into one giant ring. This trick requires important preparation.

Props needed...

* Large piece of paper
* Pencil
* Ruler
* Scissors
* Scotch tape

Preparation

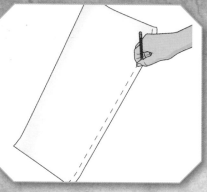

• Take your piece of paper, draw a long rectangle about 3 feet (one meter) by 2 inches (4 centimeters). Cut out the rectangle.

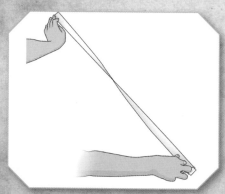

• Attach a piece of scotch tape to one end. Twist the paper once and then stick the ends together.

1 Show your audience the paper ring. Tell them that you are going to cut the ring in half to make two rings.

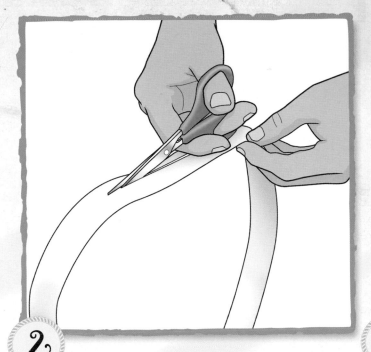

2 Cut the ring lengthwise along its middle. As long as you remember to put a twist in the ring, you will not cut it in half. It will just look as if you have.

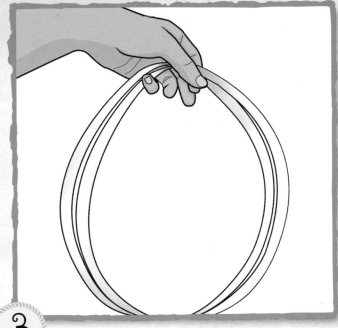

3 When you have finished, hold the paper in one hand to show that it is now two rings.

☞ **Top Tip!**

All magicians feel nervous at the start of their acts. Always begin with some easy tricks, such as this one, to build up your confidence. Make sure you practise first!

4 Tell your audience that you are now going to magically turn the two small rings into one giant ring. Wave your free hand over the rings, and say the magic word, "abracadabra."

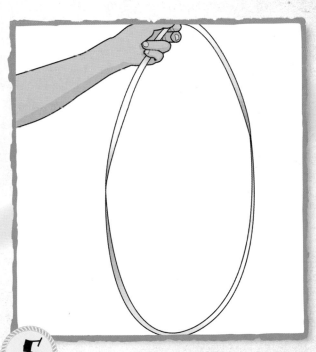

5 Now drop the first ring off the front of your fingers, the two rings will now have transformed into one large ring.

Linking rings

T his trick is mind boggling. As long as you remember to put two twists in the ring, it should work every time.

Props needed...

* Large piece of paper
* Pencil
* Ruler
* Scissors
* Scotch tape

Preparation

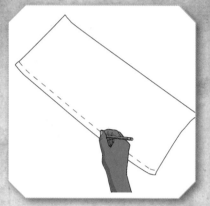

• Make a paper ring out of a long strip of paper, about 3 feet (one meter) by 2 inches (4 centimeters).

• Before you stick the ends together, twist the strip of paper twice.

1

Show your audience the paper ring. Tell them that you are going to cut the ring to make two separate rings.

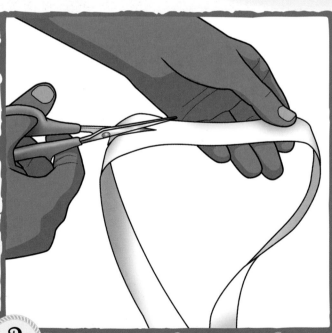

2

Cut the ring lengthwise along its middle.

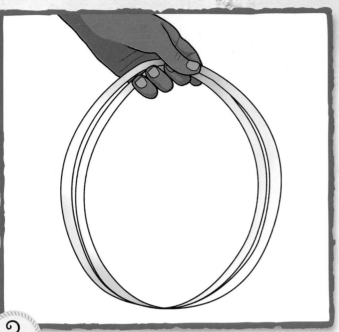

3

Once you have finished, hold the paper in one hand to show that it is now two separate rings.

4

Tell your audience that you are going to link the rings together. Wave your free hand over the rings, and say the magic word, "abracadabra."

▲ An actor stands dressed as a ghost off-stage where an assistant projects their image onto the stage using John Pepper's special effect. The actor attempts to stab the ghost with his sword but— to the audience's amazement—finds only thin air.

Pepper's ghost

Some tricks are so good, they are reused by many magicians. In the 19th century, John Pepper invented a stage illusion that used mirrors and special lighting to make objects magically appear and disappear. Today, this same illusion is used at Haunted House attractions in Disney theme parks around the world to make it look as if ghosts are appearing before the audience's eyes.

5

Now drop the first ring off the front of your fingers, while keeping hold of the other ring. The two rings will be linked together. It's magic!

The magic envelope

This great mind-reading trick is guaranteed to baffle your audience. You will need to practise the sleight of hand a few times to make sure you always pick up the card and the envelope together. If you get it wrong, your audience will see how the trick is done.

Props needed...
* Deck of cards
* Envelope
* Pen
* Piece of paper
* Table

Preparation

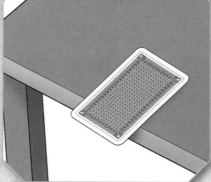

• Remove one of the cards from the deck. It does not matter which one. Write the name of the card on the piece of paper. Seal the paper inside the envelope.

• Place the card face down on the edge of the table with about one inch (2 centimeters) of it sticking out over the edge.

• Lay the envelope over the card, so the card is completely covered and part of the envelope is sticking out over the edge of the table, too.

1 Ask a volunteer to shuffle the deck of cards. Tell them that they are going to pick a card and that you have predicted which one they will choose. This is written and sealed inside the envelope.

Top Tip!
It is very important that for step 2, your volunteer does not deal the cards into a neat pile.

2 Once they have thoroughly shuffled the cards, ask your volunteer to start dealing the cards face down onto the table into a rough pile. They can stop whenever they like.

3 When they stop dealing, pick up the envelope and the card beneath it and toss them on top of the pile. It is important to do this quickly and casually, so the audience does not notice the card.

4 Ask your volunteer to open the envelope and read out your prediction.

5 Now turn over the top card, revealing that your prediction was correct!

Jumping elastic

With a simple wave of your hand, an elastic band appears to jump through the air. It is important that you prepare the elastic band in the right way, and master the sleight of hand needed to change its position.

Props needed...
* Elastic band

Preparation

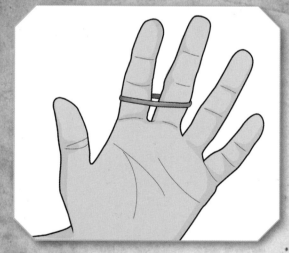

• Stretch out the fingers of your hand and wrap the elastic band around the first two fingers, below the knuckles.

• Curl your fingers into your palm and wrap the band around all four fingers, near your fingernails.

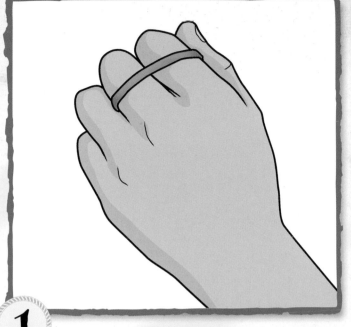

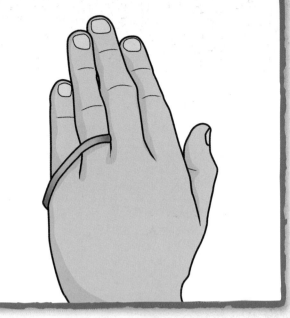

1 Show your audience the back of your hand closed in a fist. Tell them that this is a magic elastic band that can jump through the air.

2 Wave your other hand over the band, say the magic word, "abracadabra," and quickly open out all four fingers of the hand holding the band. The way you have set up elastic band will make it jump onto the other two fingers, as if by magic.

Penn and Teller

Magicians never give away their secrets, unless they are Penn and Teller that is. These two U.S. magicians have a very successful act in which they perform "impossible illusions," such as being run over by a truck. Then they reveal to their audience exactly how each trick is done.

▶ Penn and Teller's act often features dangerous looking illusions, which should never be attempted by members of the audience.

Changing spots

Props needed...
* Small dice

This trick shows that you don't need lots of big props to amaze your audience. Sometimes smaller is better. The more smoothly you can perform the sleight of hand, the more magical the trick will seem.

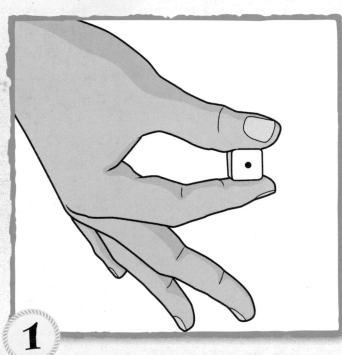

1 Pick up the dice and explain to your audience that this is a magic dice with changing spots. Hold the dice between your finger and thumb and show your audience the number on the front of the dice.

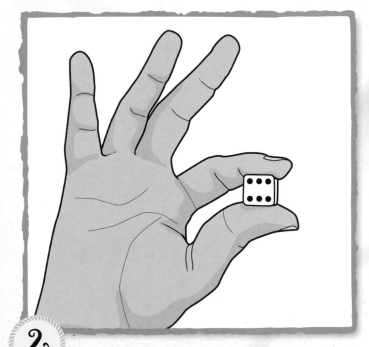

2 Turn your hand over and show the audience the number on the back of the dice.

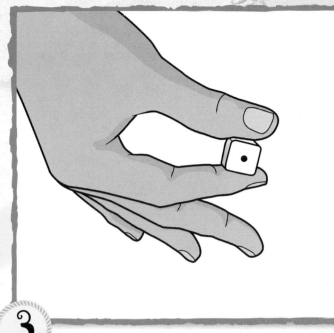

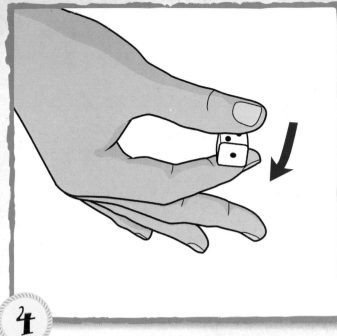

3 Turn your hand back over and show the number on the front of the dice again.

4 Wave your other hand over the dice, and say the magic word, "abracadabra." Turn over your hand, as before. This time, as you turn, use your finger and thumb to turn over the dice once. The big movement of your hand will disguise the smaller movement of your fingers.

Top Tip!

Waving your other hand over the hand that is holding the dice will distract the audience, and stop them from focusing on what you are doing.

5 Show the audience the number on the back of the dice—with your hand in the same position as step 2. The number has magically changed.

The vanishing cup

This trick uses two special skills—sleight of hand and misdirection. The audience will be concentrating so hard on the coin that they won't notice what you are actually doing.

Props needed...

* Chair
* Paper
* Plastic cup
* Table

Preparation

To perform this trick you need to be seated at a table with your legs tucked underneath.

1 Place the coin on the table and put the cup over the coin. Tell the audience that you are going to make the coin disappear.

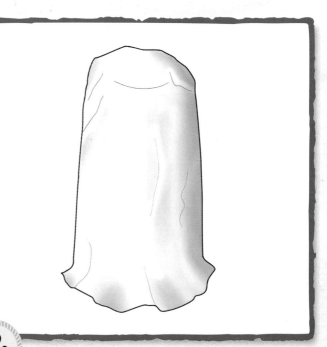

2 Now wrap a piece of paper tightly around the cup so that you can see the shape of the cup underneath.

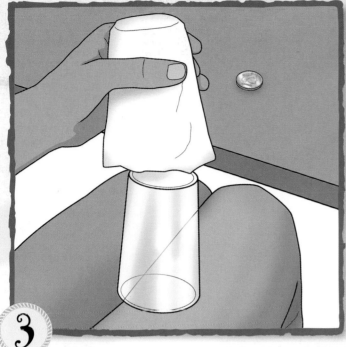

3 Lift up the cup and the paper to show the audience that the coin is still there. While they are looking at the coin, move the paper toward you to the edge of the table. Then drop the cup out of the paper into your lap. The paper should keep the shape of the cup, making it look as if it is still there.

4 Now put the cup-shaped paper back over the coin. Your audience will believe that it still contains the cup.

Top Tip!

You need to perform this sleight of hand carefully, so as not to arouse your audience's suspicions. Hopefully, the audience will be looking at the coin and won't really notice what you are doing.

5 Say the magic word, "abracadabra," and then suddenly smash down your hand on the paper, showing that the cup has vanished. Say something like "Oops, that's the problem with magic. Looks like I made the wrong thing disappear." Little do they know, you've made the right thing disappear!

Hidden hanky

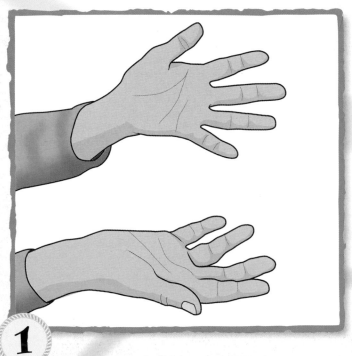

ʜaving shown your audience that there is nothing in your hands and nothing up your sleeves, you rub your hands together, say the magic words, "hey presto," and suddenly a handkerchief has appeared.

Props needed...
* Jacket or shirt with long sleeves
* Thin handkerchief

Preparation

• Fold up the handkerchief as small as it will go.

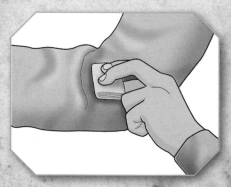

• Now push the arms of your shirt up very slightly, just an inch, so that folds begin to appear in the elbow join. Now hide the rolled-up handkerchief in one of the folds.

1

Open your hands to show the audience that there is nothing in them.

2

Roll up the sleeve of the arm not holding the handkerchief to show that you have nothing hidden there.

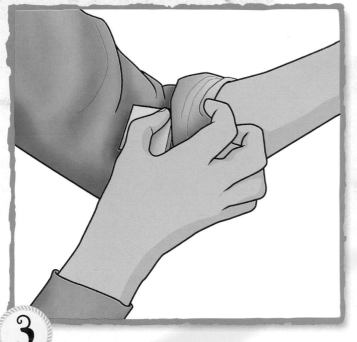

3 Then, roll up the sleeve of the arm holding the handkerchief. Now for the sleight of hand—use your thumb to quickly move the handkerchief from its fold into the palm of your hand.

4 Keeping the handkerchief hidden in your palm, rub your hands together to open up the handkerchief. Then magically produce the handkerchief, as if from nowhere.

Top Tip!

For the best results, the handkerchief should be the same color as the shirt you are wearing during the trick.

Chinese water torture cell

This was the name given to a very famous trick performed by one of the most famous magicians in the world, Harry Houdini. In it, Houdini had his feet bound in metal cuffs, before being hung upside down in a tank filled with water. Drapes were then drawn in front of the tank, hiding Houdini from his audience. After a pause to build up the tension, the magician would then escape, free and unhurt!

▶ In 2002, Criss Angel put a new spin on Harry Houdini's trick when he spent 24 hours upside-down inside a water-filled tank.

Going, going, gone

You show your audience a coin and announce that you are going to make it melt through the table. You place the coin flat on the table, and start rubbing its top with your finger. Amazingly, the coin starts to disappear!

Props needed...
* Coin
* Table

Top Tip!

Practise talking to your audience. If you are going to tell jokes, make sure you memorize them. The more confident you are, the more your audience will enjoy your performance.

1 Sit at the table with your legs tucked well underneath.

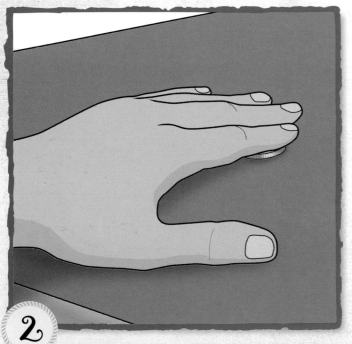

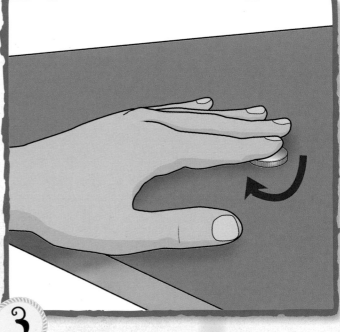

2 Put your hand out flat, with your wrist on the edge of the table. Extend all four fingers and keep them held tightly together. Place the coin on the table, under your first finger.

3 Keep your hand in this position as you begin to rub the top of the coin, using small circular movements.

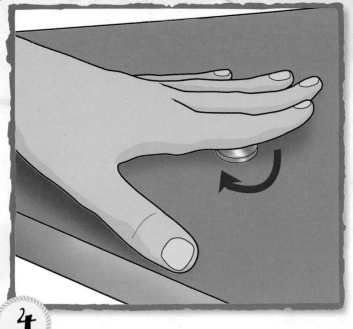

Let the coin fall
into your lap

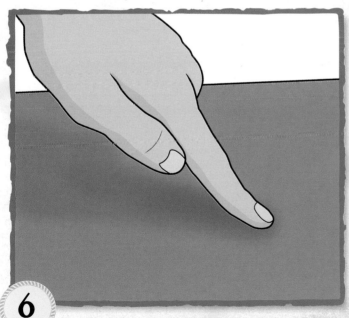

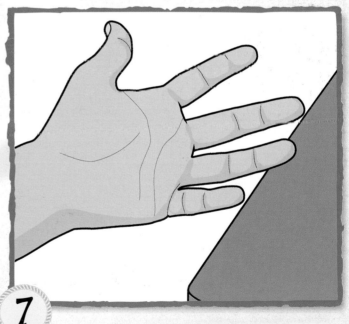

4 After a few rubs, start moving the coin backward under your hand, out of sight of the audience.

5 Keep rubbing your finger on the table, as if the coin were still there, all the time using the motion of your hand to move the coin backward. Once it gets to the back of your hand, allow the coin to slip off the table into your lap.

6 Once the coin is in your lap, raise your hand in the air and press the tip of your first finger onto the table. Make a final few rubs, so it looks like you are getting rid of the last of the coin.

7 Lift your hand to show that the coin has completely disappeared. Magic!

The hand pass

This trick is all about speed and accuracy, and will take practise to get right. The result, however, is guaranteed to puzzle your audience.

Props needed...
* Coin

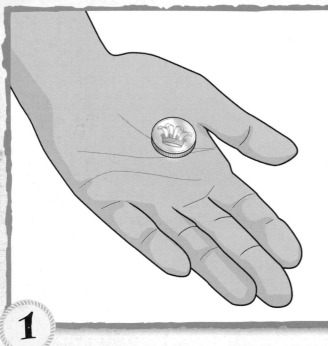

1 Place the coin into the palm of your hand, near the thumb.

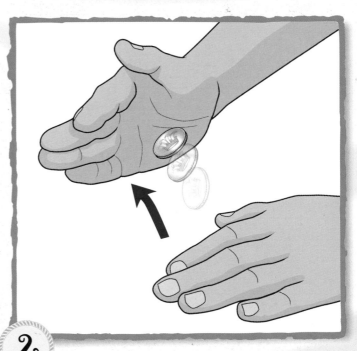

2 This is the tricky bit. Quickly turn over both hands. You are going to flick the coin from one hand under the other. Make sure you turn the hand catching the coin just after the hand flipping the coin, so that there is room for it to go under.

Top Tip!

It is best to perform this trick on a soft surface, so that the coin will not make a noise when it lands.

3 Ask a volunteer to say which hand the coin is under. They obviously pick the hand they last saw the coin in.

4 They are, of course, wrong. You turn over your hands over to reveal that the coin has magically switched hands.

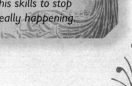

Misdirecting the audience

Whether big or small, all tricks rely on the audience not noticing what is really going on. One way of fooling the audience is to use sleight of hand. Another is to employ a technique called misdirection. This means doing lots of things that have nothing to do with the trick, such as telling jokes or waving a wand. This distracts the audience's attention and directs them away from the secrets of the magic.

◀ *Lance Burton performs the famous "sawing a woman in half" trick live on U.S. television. Of course, the woman is not really harmed. The magician uses his skills to stop the audience from working out what is really happening.*

Hole in the head

This is all about smoothness and timing. To fool your audience, you will have to get the performance of this piece of sleight of hand just right.

Props needed...
* Small sponge ball

1 Pick up a sponge ball and place it in the center of your hand.

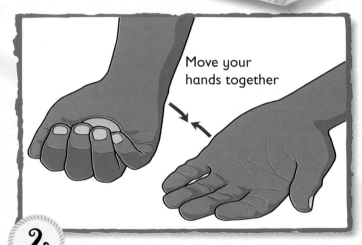

Move your hands together

2 Keeping both hands palm up, start moving your hands together. As you do, start curling the fingers of the hand holding the ball toward you.

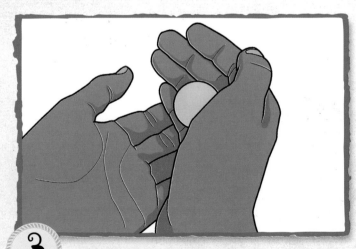

3 When your hands are close together, move the hand not holding the ball in front of the other hand. This will hide the ball from the audience.

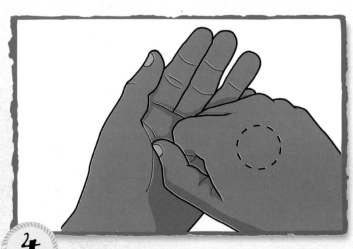

4 Now turn over the hand holding the ball.

90

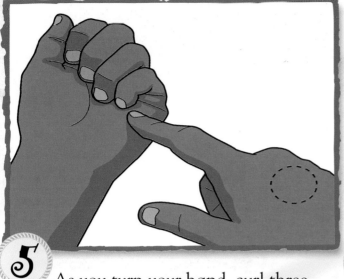

5 As you turn your hand, curl three of your fingers around the ball. At the same time, curl all of the fingers of your other hand toward your palm as if you have just taken hold of the ball.

6 With your empty hand, which the audience believes is now holding the ball, tap yourself lightly on the head.

7 As you tap yourself, raise the hand that is actually holding the ball up to your mouth.

8 Put your hand over your mouth and pretend to cough. Bring your hand away, showing that it now contains the ball. It will look like the ball has traveled right through your head!

Birds from thin air

Channing Pollock was a U.S. magician who could perform many clever tricks using cards and handkerchiefs. However, he became famous above all for one particular illusion—his ability to produce live doves "from the air." Pollock eventually left his career as a magician to become an actor in Hollywood.

▶ Channing Pollock displays his amazing sleight of hand with a pack of cards. He was one of the most skillful magicians of his day.

The seven principles

The magicians Penn and Teller are well known for explaining the secrets behind their tricks.

According to them, all sleight-of-hand tricks rely on the same skills, which they call the "seven principles of sleight of hand." They have one particular illusion that they use to demonstrate these skills. In the trick, Teller appears to repeatedly get rid of a small object and then get a new one. However, it is then revealed that he is actually using the same object the whole time! Penn explains the principles while Teller performs.

The seven principles are…

Ditch
To secretly remove an object that is no longer needed.

Load
To secretly move an object to where it is needed.

Misdirection
To direct attention away from what you are actually doing.

Palm
To hold an object in a hand that seems empty.

Simulation
To make it appear that something has happened when it actually hasn't.

Steal
To secretly get an object that is needed.

Switch
To secretly swap one object for another.

▲ *Penn (center) and Teller (left) receive an award to celebrate performing their magic show in Las Vegas for five years.*

MIND TRICKS

Change the arrow

Use water to magically change the direction of the arrow. This trick is simple, but very impressive.

Preparation

• Before facing your audience, place your card and glass on the table.

• Fold the card in half. On one side of the card, draw an arrow. It should be just shorter than the width of your glass.

1 Stand your folded piece of card on the table with the arrow facing the audience.

Now challenge your audience to make the arrow change direction without touching the paper or glass.

2 Place a glass in front of the arrow, so the arrow can be clearly seen through the glass.

Making the Statue of Liberty disappear

In 1983, the magician David Copperfield performed one of the most amazing illusions of all time when he made the 305-foot (93-meter) Statue of Liberty disappear in front of a New York audience. No one knows for sure how the did it, but some people believe the audience were sat on a revolving turntable. When the statue was briefly hidden behind drapes, the turntable turned away from the statue. The curtain was then dropped, revealing empty space.

▶ The "reappeared" Statue of Liberty—David Copperfield has never told anyone how he made it "vanish."

4 When they give up, produce your hidden jug of water and pour it into the glass. The arrow will appear to change direction. Pouring the water will turn the glass into a lens and, from the audience's viewpoint, change the direction of the arrow.

The magic lunch

Performed well, these two tricks will make your friends think that you have a magic genie in your lunchbox.

Props needed...
* Banana
* Lunchbox
* Needle and thread

Preparation

* Push the threaded needle into one of the ridges and out through the next ridge.

* Push the needle back into the second hole and out through the third ridge. Make sure a loop of thread hangs out of the banana.

* Repeat until you've been all the way round. Then pull both ends of thread out through the first hole and this will slice the banana. Repeat as many times as you like.

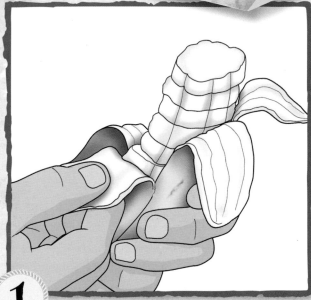

1 Tell your friend that you think you have a "genie" in your lunchbox. To prove it, open your lunchbox and hand your friend the banana. Ask them to peel it. The banana will come apart in slices in their hands. The genie did it!

Top Tip!

The more you act as if what you are doing is "magic" and not part of a trick, the more your audience will believe you.

Preparation

Place your glass bottle of soda in the refrigerator for several hours so that it is very cold.

Props needed...

* Soda in a glass bottle
* Lunchbox
* Small coin

1 Take the bottle of soda out of your lunchbox. Open it and hand it to your friend and tell them that the genie is trying to get out. Put the coin on top of the bottle to keep the genie in.

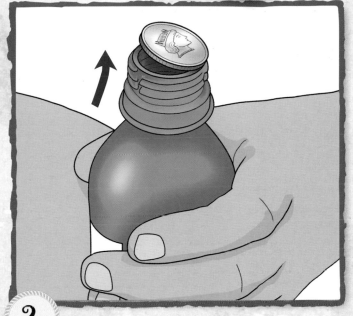

2 Tell your friend to hold onto the bottle with both hands. After a while, the coin will pop up slightly, "letting the genie out." As long as the bottle is cold enough, the warmth of your friend's hands will cause the gas inside the bottle to expand, pushing the coin up.

Crazy stunts

Criss Angel often performs amazing stunts to a shocked audience! He has been run over by a steamroller while laying on a bed of glass, and even escaped being hit by a speeding car— while chained to a parked car full of explosives. Criss sometimes reveals to his fans how his illusions are done.

▶ In 2002, Criss Angel hung from eight fish-hooks for nearly six hours!

Finger magnets

★ ★

This fascinating routine uses a very important mind trick technique—the power of suggestion. You will make your volunteer believe that something natural is happening by the power of magic!

Props needed...
* Watch

1

Ask a volunteer if you can hypnotize them. Tell them that it is safe and the effect will only last for a couple of minutes.

2

Now pretend to hypnotize them. Wave a watch in front of them and ask them to follow it with their eyes.

3

Now, ask them to clasp their hands together.

4

Keeping their other fingers together, ask them to stick up their first fingers.

Using magic to end a war

In the 19th century, France controlled the African country of Algeria. Fearing that the people there were going to start a war against them, the French government sent the magician Robert-Houdin to Algeria. He performed many amazing magic tricks, including catching a bullet between his teeth, which made the Algerian people believe that he had magic powers. This made them give up their plans for war.

▶ Feathers fly as Robert-Houdin, the "magician who stopped a war" performs one of his many amazing tricks.

5
Tell your volunteer that when you hypnotized them, you magnetized their fingers. Wave your hands over their fingers and tell them that no matter how hard they try to keep their first fingers apart, the magnetism will draw them together.

Top Tip!
Tell jokes or stories while doing your trick to misdirect, or distract, your audience from what you're actually doing. Then they won't work out how the trick is done!

6
Watch as your volunteer's fingers slowly start moving together. As you have told them that they are hypnotized, they will think that is why their fingers are touching. In fact, when held in this position, your fingers will naturally come together.

The rising ring

★ ★ ★

Watch in amazement as the ring seems to defy gravity with this simple trick.

Props needed...
* Elastic band
* Metal ring

Preparation
Cut your elastic band so that it is a single length of elastic.

Top Tip!
When performing a trick, try to appear confident. Act as if you know exactly what you are doing, even if you don't. The more nervous you seem, the more the audience will feel that you are trying to trick them.

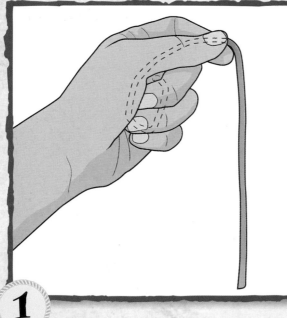

1

For this trick to work, you need to pick up the elastic band in a certain way. With one hand, take hold of the band about halfway down, so that half of the band is hidden in your palm.

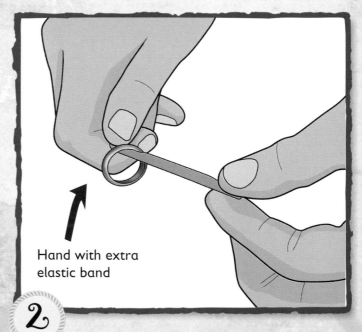

Hand with extra elastic band

2

With your other hand, thread the ring onto the loose end of the band.

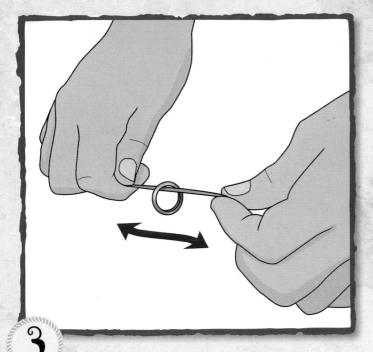

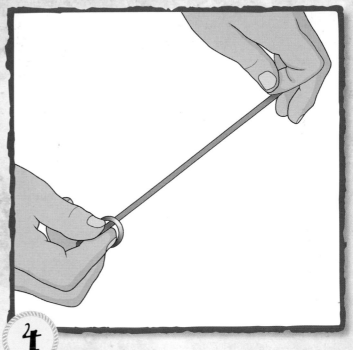

3 Grip the loose end of the band and pull it taut. Show the audience that there is nothing suspicious about the ring by raising and lowering your hands to slide the ring up and down.

4 Announce that you are going to make the ring defy gravity. The ring should rest against the hand hiding the length of elastic. Lift your other hand so that the band is now stretched into a slight slope.

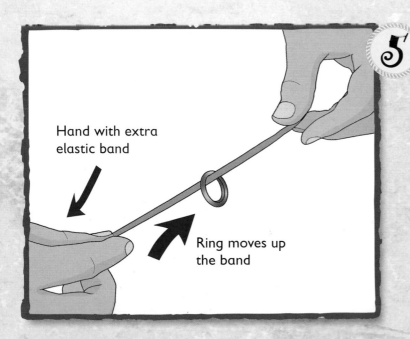

Hand with extra elastic band

Ring moves up the band

5 Now for the tricky bit. Slowly and carefully, let the length of elastic band gathered in your hand slip through your finger and thumb. This will make it look like the ring is magically sliding up the band. In fact, it is being carried upward by the elastic band, although your audience will not notice this.

Crazy cups

Here is a trick guaranteed to drive your audience crazy. As simple as it looks, no matter how hard they try, they just will not be able to get it to work.

Props needed...
* Three cups

Preparation

Set up the cups in this way.

A   B   C

1

Tell a volunteer that you want them to turn the cups the right way up. Explain that they can turn them just three times, and that each time they must turn two cups at once, one with each hand. First, show your volunteer how it is done.

B   C

2 Turn over cups B and C.

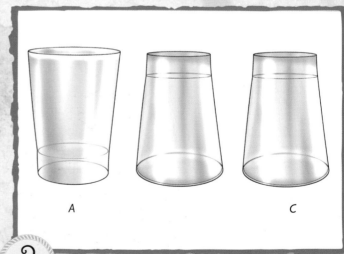

A   C

3 Turn over cups A and C.

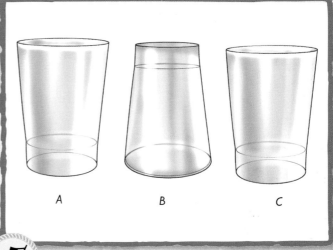

Top Tip!

Make sure you set up the cups for your friend as quickly and as casually as possible, so they cannot see that you are tricking them. Once you have completed step 4, you only need to turn over the middle cup.

4 Turn over cups B and C again.

5 Now reset the cups for your volunteer to try the trick. However, when you set up the cups for them, you are going to do it slightly differently. Although it may look similar, the way you set up the cups for your volunteer is in fact opposite to the way you do it for yourself.

The heaviest box

In his stage act, the 19th-century magician Robert-Houdin would get a child to pick up a lightweight metal box. He would then challenge a strong man from the audience to do the same. When the man was unable to lift it, Houdin would claim it was because he had used magic to make them lose their strength. In fact, he had secretly turned on a powerful magnet, which held the box to the floor.

▶ Robert-Houdin often used his son in his act, as in this levitation trick.

103

The magic toothpicks

You will need to gather your audience around you to perform this trick—you will not be able to move your props once they are set up.

Preparation

• Take a toothpick and dip it in dishwashing liquid. Allow it to dry and then place it in your pocket.

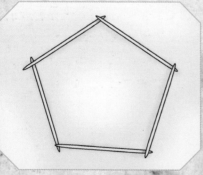

• Fill your bowl with water. On the surface of the water, balance five toothpicks, so that they form a five-sided shape called a pentagon.

Top Tip!

Practise this trick plenty of times before attempting to do it in public.

1 Ask your audience to stand close to you so they can clearly see the toothpicks floating in the bowl.

2 Tell your audience that you are going to use the power of your mind to make the toothpicks break apart.

3

Take out the prepared soapy toothpick from your pocket, and touch it on the surface of the water in the center of the toothpicks.

4

After a few seconds, the toothpicks forming the pentagon will begin to float away from each other.

5

Make the toothpick pentagon again and invite a volunteer to try to break it apart. Without the special soapy toothpick, they will not be able to. The dishwashing liquid on the toothpick causes a thin film of soap to form on the surface of the water. When it reaches the pentagon, the soap breaks apart the water molecules holding the toothpicks in position.

Mind magician

Derren Brown is a mind magician who uses mind-control skills and hypnotism to make people perform extraordinary acts. In his shows, he has convinced someone that they were living inside a video game, made a group of people rob a bank, and put a member of the public into a trance in one country, and then woken them up in another.

▶ Look into his eyes—Derren Brown is one of the most popular mind magicians performing today.

Magic number nine

You are going to use a clever piece of preparation to make it look as if you have read the mind of your subject. As long as your volunteer works out their sums correctly, this trick should work every time.

Preparation

For the best results, this trick should be performed in a casual setting, such as a living room, where there are books and magazines. Before you start the trick, choose a book or magazine, turn to page nine, and memorize the first word.

Speed magic

Hans Klok is a Dutch magician who regularly performs in Las Vegas, the "world capital of magic." He claims to be the fastest magician in the world, and packs dozens of tricks into his act, including levitation, sawing a woman in half, and making a light bulb magically float over an audience.

▶ In his act, Hans Klok performs an illusion in which he appears to separate someone's head from their body.

1 Tell your friend that you are going to read their mind. Give them a pencil, a piece of paper, and a calculator to work out any sums.

a) 4217

b) 1472

c) 4217 − 1472 = 2745

d) 2 + 7 + 4 + 5 = 18

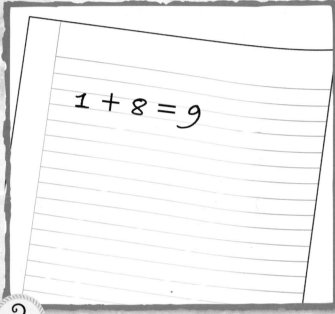

$1 + 8 = 9$

2 a) Ask your volunteer to think of a four-digit number and write it down.
b) Rearrange those four digits to make another four-digit number. Write that down as well.
c) Using the calculator, subtract the smaller number from the larger number. Write the new number down.
d) Add the four separate digits of the new number together.

3 Ask your volunteer if they have a one-digit or two-digit number. If they have a two-digit number, they need to add the digits together so they end up with a one-digit number.

4 Now ask your friend to pick up your prepared book. Ask them to turn to the page matching their final number and to memorize the first word on that page.

5 Pretend to concentrate deeply for a few moments, and then write down the word on a piece of paper and hand it to the volunteer. The secret is the number will always be nine, so you will never be wrong!

it all adds up

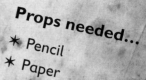

This trick is all about the words you use when talking to your volunteer. Make sure you follow the instructions carefully, then sit back and watch them fall into your mathematical trap.

Props needed...
* Pencil
* Paper

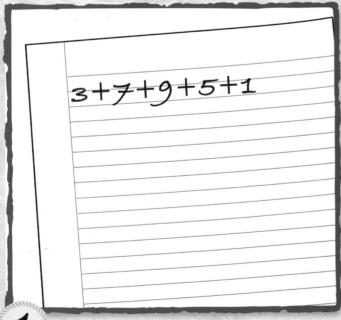

$$3+7+9+5+1$$

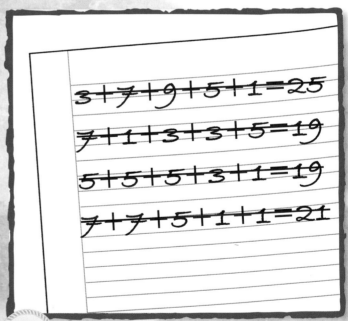

$$3+7+9+5+1=25$$
$$7+1+3+3+5=19$$
$$5+5+5+3+1=19$$
$$7+7+5+1+1=21$$

1 Give your friend or volunteer a piece of paper and a pencil. Tell them to write down five odd figures (under 20) that will add up to 20.

2 20 is an even number. Try as they might, your volunteer will not be able to add odd figures up to total 20. Now it's the magician's turn.

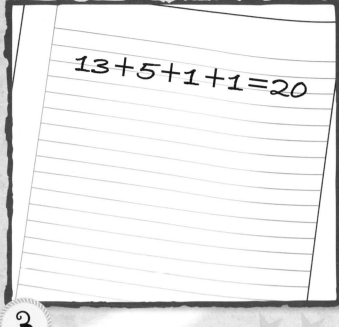

$$13+5+1+1=20$$

13—2 figures
5—1 figure
1—1 figure
1—1 figure

3 On the paper, write down the numbers 13, 5, 1, and 1, then add them up. The total will be 20.

4 When your volunteer points out that you have only used four odd numbers, simply explain that although there are only four odd numbers, there are actually five odd figures.

5 By using using the word "figure," you will trick your volunteer into writing down five numbers.

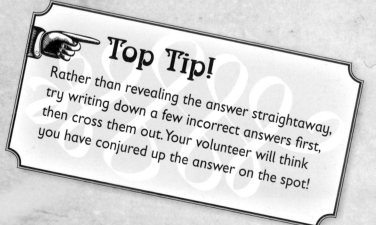

Top Tip!
Rather than revealing the answer straightaway, try writing down a few incorrect answers first, then cross them out. Your volunteer will think you have conjured up the answer on the spot!

The nose never lies

This trick may not work every single time, but it should work often enough to convince people of your magical powers.

Roller coaster ride

In 1999, U.S. magician Lance Burton performed a death-defying trick when he had himself handcuffed to the tracks of a roller coaster. Traveling up to 80 miles (130 kilometers) an hour, a roller coaster was set in motion on the track, giving Burton one minute to set himself free. He escaped with just a tenth of a second to spare.

▼ *Lance Burton performs another daring feat of escapology—breaking free from a straitjacket during one of his shows.*

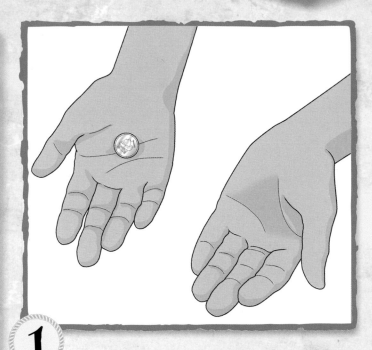

1 Ask your friend or volunteer to put a coin in one of their hands.

2 Now ask them to put their hands behind their back, place the coin into whichever hand they want, and close their fist over it.

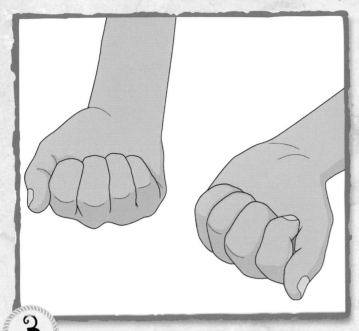

3 Ask them to put their closed hands in front of them. Look closely for a visual clue, which magicians call a "tell"— a movement made by your volunteer, which lets you know where something is. Most people point their nose slightly toward whichever hand the coin is in.

4 Pretend to read their mind, then tell them which hand the coin is hidden in.

5 If you have got it right, your volunteer will be impressed, but of course, it could just be luck. So you need to do the trick a few times. As long as your volunteer is doing what you want them to do, this trick should keep working.

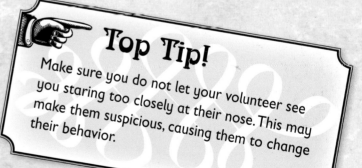

Top Tip!
Make sure you do not let your volunteer see you staring too closely at their nose. This may make them suspicious, causing them to change their behavior.

Heads or tails?

Tell your friend, or better a group of friends, that you can predict if a coin is showing heads or tails when it is hidden beneath one of their hands.

Props needed...
* Six coins

1

Give your friends six coins, or even better, get them to provide their own six coins. If they use their own coins, they cannot think that you are using "magic coins."

2

Ask one of your friends to throw the coins onto a table so they land with some of the coins showing heads and some showing tails. If they all show heads or tails, ask them to do it again.

3

Silently count how many coins are showing heads, and note whether it is an odd number or an even number.

4

Turn your back and ask your friend to pick one coin with their left hand and one with their right hand and to turn over the coins. Tell them that they can do this with as many pairs of coins as they like, as many times as they like.

Top Tip!

Because you have a 50–50 chance of getting this right, this trick gets more impressive the more times you repeat it.

5 When they have finished turning over the coins, ask them to cover up one coin with their hand.

6 Turn back, and again make a mental note of how many of the coins are showing heads, and whether it is an odd number or an even number.

7 a) Now for the tricky bit. If you saw an odd number of heads at the beginning and it is still an odd number, or if you saw an even number and it is still an even number, the coin under the hand will be tails.

b) If the number of heads has changed, from odd to even, or from even to odd, the coin under the hand will be heads.

Face up, face down

Props needed...
* Deck of playing cards
* Table

This mind-reading trick takes quite a bit of concentration from both you and your volunteer, but it will have a big impact.

1 Ask your volunteer to hold the deck of cards face down.

2 Turn your back and ask your volunteer to count out between ten and 30 cards face up. They should remember how many cards they have dealt.

3 Your volunteer should now have two piles of cards—one face down and one face up. With your back still turned, ask them to mix the face up cards into the face down pile. They can shuffle the cards as many times as they like.

4   Your volunteer should now be holding one pile of cards—some face up, some face down. Ask them to remember how many cards they dealt out at the start of the trick and then deal out the same number of cards again.

5   Tell them to pick up the pile they have just dealt and to turn their back. Ask them to count how many of the cards in their deck are face down, but not to tell you because you are going to read their mind to find out the number.

6   Turn back to your volunteer and pick up the other pile. Silently count how many face up cards there are. If your volunteer has followed the stages correctly, the number of face up cards in your pile will be exactly the same as the number of face down cards in their pile.

7   Put down your pile, take your time to build up the tension, and then reveal the number.

The magic crayon

This X-ray vision trick needs your best acting skills—and will only work if you don't bite your nails!

Props needed...
* Packet of wax crayons

1 Hand your volunteer the wax crayons. Tell them that you can "see" colors through your fingers and you are going to tell them which color crayon they have chosen without looking.

2 Turn away from the volunteer and put your hands behind your back.

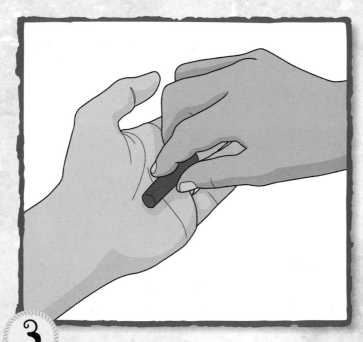

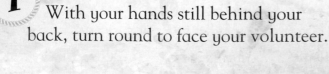

3 Ask your volunteer to pick any color crayon they want and to place it into one of your hands.

5 Now, use one of the nails on your other hand to scrape off a tiny amount of crayon with your nail.

4 With your hands still behind your back, turn round to face your volunteer.

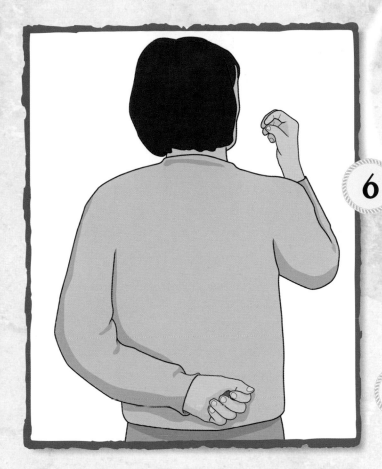

Top Tip!

Telling jokes and stories will make your performance fun and distract your audience from working out what you are doing.

6 Keep the hand holding the crayon behind your back and bring the other hand up to your forehead, as if you are trying to concentrate. Curl the fingers inward and you will be able to quickly glance at the piece of crayon beneath your nail.

7 After a short pause to build up the tension, reveal the color of the crayon.

Magic in the air

Wouter Bijendijk—who performs under the stage name "Ramana" —is a renowned magician from Holland. He is particularly well known for his feats of levitation —making objects fly through the air and even appearing to hover more than 3 feet (one meter) above the ground himself.

▶ Ramana's levitation act seems particularly impressive because he often does it out on the streets, so people can see he is not using strings or wires.

The chair lift

Props needed...
* Stool

Reveal your friends' hidden strength with this great hands-on trick. You will need an audience for this trick because five people will take part.

1 Ask a volunteer to sit on the stool. Arrange the other four people next to them—two on the right-hand side, and two on the left-hand side.

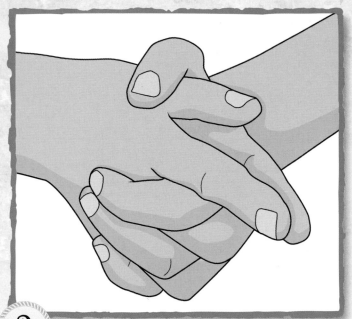

2 Ask the four standing people to clasp their hands together and to point their index fingers forward. Tell them that they are going to try to lift the sitter into the air just using their fingers. Make it clear that you don't think this will work.

3 Two people should put their fingers in the sitter's armpits, and the other two should put their fingers behind the sitter's knees.

4 Now ask them to try to lift the sitter. They will soon find that it is impossible.

6 Wave your hand in front of the sitter's face and tell them that you are using hypnotism to make them lighter.

7 Tell the lifters that you are going to count to three. When you get to three you want them to quickly take their hands off the sitter and to try to lift them again.

5 Now tell the sitter that you are going to use mind magic to make them lighter. Ask the four lifters to all gently place their hands on top of the sitter's head.

Here's how it's done...

Penn and Teller are a special type of double act. Not only do they perform numerous clever illusions, they also spend part of each performance showing the audience exactly how some of their tricks are done.

▼ They may look dangerous, but Penn and Teller's tricks are carefully rehearsed so that neither of them get hurt.

8 Count to three, they start to lift and, "hey presto," the sitter is suddenly up in the air. By telling people that they can do this trick, it makes them believe that they can, so they will try harder without realizing! Also, as they are trying the second attempt at speed, they will be using more force.

The Balducci Levitation

ere is a quick piece of mind magic you can do, known as the Balducci Levitation. Performed well, it will look to a spectator as if you have hovered in mid air for a few seconds.

1 Get your spectator to stand behind you at around a 45-degree angle. Lift the foot closest to the spectator into the air by a couple of inches.

2 At the same time, stand on the tiptoe of the other foot and lift the heel into the air by a couple of inches. You'll now look as if you are floating!